The Runes:
A Deeper Journey

by Kari C. Tauring

edited by David de Young

The Runes: A Deeper Journey

Copyright © 2016 by Kari C. Tauring

Based on The Runes: A Human Journey Copyright ©2007 by Kari C. Tauring

Kari C. Tauring, MA, volva
Minneapolis, MN
kari@karitauring.com
KariTauring.com

Cover art and design by Felicitas Maria Sokec.

The rune images used in this book are in the public domain.

Published by Nordic Moon Press, Finland
www.nordicmoonpress.com
Printed by Lulu.com in the United States of America.

ISBN: 978-1-387-65560-1

Contents

The Elder Futhark:

Freyr/Freya's Aett

ᚠ Fehu – letter/sound F - Domestic Animals

ᚢ Uruz – letter/sound U/oo - Wild Ox

ᚦ Thurisaz – letters/sound TH - Giants

ᚨ Ansuz – letter/sound A/ah - Mouth

ᚱ Raido – letter/sound R - Wheel

ᚲ Kenaz – letter/sound K/C hard c - Torch

ᚷ Gebo – letter/sound G soft g - Gift

ᚹ Wunjo – letter/sound W - Joy

Heimdal/Hela's Aett

ᚺ Hagalaz – letter/sound H - Hail

ᚾ Naudiz – letter/sound N - Need

ᛁ Isaz – letter/sound I/eee - Ice

ᛃ Jera – letter/sound J/yuh - Year

ᛇ Eiwaz – letter/sound Y/ye - Yew

ᛈ Perth – letter/sound P - Luck

ᛉ Algiz – letter/sound Z - Elk

ᛋ Sowilo – letter/sound S - Sun

Tyr/Zisa's Aett

↑ Tiwaz – letter/sound T - God

ᛒ Berkanan – letter/sound B - Birch

ᛗ Ehwaz – letter/sound E/eh - Horse

ᛗ Mannaz – letter/sound M - Community

Γ Laguz – letter/sound L - Lake

ᛜ Ingwaz – letters/sounds ING - Lord

ᛞ Dagaz – letter/sound D – Day

ᛟ Othila – letter/sound O – Homeland

Photo by Karin Odell
2007

Making Runes

*I still use the runes I made from my own Buckthorn.
Using felled trees honors and gives them a sacred life.*

Introduction by David de Young

My first encounter with the runes was in the late 1990s, and after working with my first set for a while, I was excited to find the runes cut a deeper swathe for me than other forms of divination I had studied. They resonated with an ancient tone that contributed to a new-found appreciation of archetypal values – too often forgotten in modern times – that are the bedrock of a successful human community.

Many books on runes I had read took an historical approach. Others took what struck me as an over-simplified cut, providing information without mythological context. I sought a book that could be used for divination, but which could also be read to develop a deeper understanding of the spiritual path, or "red road" in the Native American tradition, a life of truth, friendship, respect for the self and others, and community service.

My friend and fellow musician Kari Tauring had given me rune readings which revealed the historical, mythic, and magical meanings of the runes. Kari's readings were born of an ancient understanding yet had up-to-the-minute applicability. I asked her if she would consider writing down what she knew, and the result is the book you have in your hands.

The approach we took to creating this book was that Kari pulled a rune daily and wrote about it as it seemed to apply to the day it was selected. After her first series of pulls, my editing followed the same process: I pulled a rune and applied my focus to it on that particular day. This methodology caused this book to come alive for us long before the first edition was complete. As I worked through issues in my life during the spring of 2006 and through the many subsequent drafts of each rune entry, I felt I was harnessing the power of all the runes at once, like a reading that ultimately included the runes of all three aettir.

When we placed the edited rune entries into the Elder Futhark order we follow in this text, I had an epiphany. Though the book had been written in seemingly random order, the runes by their very nature were still inclined to fall into their Futhark sequence. The relationships among them became clear, and I saw how they flowed one to the next almost as if I had figured it out for myself.

In the entry for Mannaz (also called Mannheim), Kari writes: "When you draw Mannheim, look around to see who is supporting you and in what ways they are doing so. Find the community network that feeds your highest good and see what you can contribute to it." This book is both a product of community and, we hope, a contribution to it. If you see yourself in any of the entries that follow, it is because your stories and traditions and those of your loved ones, past and present, had a hand in its creation as well.

Minneapolis, August 2006

Revised – Helsinki, Finland, August 2016

Preface by Kari Tauring

The Indo-European word rune comes from the Sanskrit word ru meaning secret conversation or whispered mystery. The pre-Vedic god Rudra was the force of wind and the howling of nature's secret mysteries, a red-haired howling sky god. Runes are the symbols of nature energies and poetic spells to put humans into deeper relationship with nature entities. The Finno-Ugric word runo comes from the same root. Runos are nature magical poems which are sung as well as the poet magician who sings them. Both runes and runos have a special meter, assonance, alliteration, and imitate the sounds of nature. The users of runes and runos are considered magicians, healers, and priest/esses.

As visual symbols, the Elder Futhark of Germanic Runes shares characteristics with the Hungarian rune alphabet, the Etruscan rune alphabet, and the alphabet of the Phoenicians, a trading culture whose influence and language ranged from the middle east to Sweden, to possibly even Ohio in the USA! The Phoenicians are credited with inventing the phonemic alphabet, the ship's keel, the oar, and a rare, expensive indigo dye. Many scholars believe it was a group related to the Phoenicians who brought sheep, goats, horses, agriculture and metallurgy north from Iran, instigating the Scandinavian Bronze Age in circa 2000 BCE.

The similarities between the scriptural symbol systems may have been partly the result of the constraints of the materials – clay, rock, wood, bone, metal – upon which they were inscribed. But also, the shapes tend to echo similar natural landscapes of lakes, rivers, ice, cattle, horses, and trees. The concepts behind the runes arose from cultures that honored herds of cattle both wild and domestic; bones and relics have been found dating to 30,000 BC and public art in France and Spain as old as 16,000 years has been discovered that illustrates these concepts. It is interesting to note that the first letter of all the Indo-European languages holds the meaning of ox or cow.

The runes were also a product of the cultures of the Northern continent which held Birch as sacred, and cultures that honor hard work, community, and voluntary reciprocity. The runes tell a story of unity and migration, individuation and revelation. They provide us with a roadmap that helps us to find our way back to one another. All cultures and the stories they tell are connected at the core by this psychological truth: humans are always in relationship to each other. After all, what is a secret conversation without a listener to respond?

The Germanic tribes were reported by Tacitus (Roman historian) to be scribing symbols on twigs and casting them for divination as early as the 40s BC. The rune alphabet changed with the languages and was used well into the European Middle Age. In Minnesota, we have an example of a rune stone (authenticity still debated) which dates itself to 1362. I am using the Elder Futhark, the earliest complete rune alphabet on written record dating to around 100 AD. I reference the Norwegian, Icelandic and Anglo-Saxon rune poems written, likely, as mnemonic devices between the 8th and 15th centuries AD.

The influence of Christianity on the interpretation of the runes and mythology has been profound. We owe the very existence of Germanic/Nordic runes to the fact that the Romans never occupied Scandinavia. The Romans generally placed their culture on top of whomever they were conquering that day. In addition, the Norse were an oral tradition culture and didn't use the runes as a written alphabet as a rule. Emperor Theodosius of Rome initiated a ban on pagan practices including alphabets in 389 A.D. but Christian Rome didn't have great influence in Scandinavia until late in the Viking Era (1000 AD). For this reason, we still have poems and histories written in runes from the Middle Ages.

After Christianization, rune knowledge and runic script went underground and was practiced within family traditions and secret societies. Those caught attempting to perpetuate rune lore in public were subject to punishment by death (or worse). Knowledge, stories, cultural values and spiritual traditions forced underground due to persecution of their practitioners tend to become distorted and to reflect the dysfunction of oppression. Much of the Nordic spiritual lore was hidden in the folk songs and fairy tales, relegated to "children's nonsense" and "old wives' tales," preserved there to be mined by descendants like me.

While I strive to maintain a pre-Christian Nordic cultural mindset, I also relate to the runes through the filter of modern female. Through my work in the arts, I have attempted to present balanced relationships between our male and female sides, our humanity and our divinity, and our need for community. I also relate these stories as a mother, attempting to teach this knowledge to the next generation with the distortions and dysfunctions explained and hopefully eliminated. There are plenty of books that will tell you how to use the runes for cursing and dark magic. That's just not me. I believe that we attract what we put out - so this book is about healing, growing, and discovering the roots of Nordic öorlog. In divination, the first pre-Christian mindset is to realize that there is no future tense. Rune reversals are asking questions such as: Are you looking into the roots or the branches? Are you are looking at the reflection of the rune in the well? What are you reminded to do by this reversed image to make it right again?

The runes are symbols with sounds and meanings that exist deep within our ancient memory. They are programmed into our genetic code, remembered by our reptilian brains and flow in our very blood. They have always been and will always be relevant.

I never intended to write a rune book. Instead, I undertook the writing of "The Runes: A Human Journey" in 2006 as a favor to David de Young who devised the writing ritual and edited the book with great care and devotion. When I asked, "Why do you want me to write a rune book? There are so many already!" He said, "Yes, but I want yours. None of them tell the personal stories of the runes the way you do." That has been the basis of the popularity for this book over the years. It is academic yet accessible, universal yet personal. I never expected it to sell as well as it has, and I never would have guessed it would also spawn a popular rune application for iPhone. (In fact, I didn't even know what an iPhone "app" was until 2010 when I designed ours!)

Three issues surfaced after the first edition was published in 2007, and the second edition means to correct them. First, people wanted the "Roman Alphabet" correspondence to the runes represented so they could use the runes for writing scripts and spelling their names. Second, I chose rune pronunciations from all of the poems in a way only consistent with my tastes. Third, I felt a strong need to expand the "divination" section because I really wanted people to understand what divination means from a Norse perspective.

The first issue was easily solved by adding the Roman alphabet equivalent to the rune chart in the front of the book and in the beginning of each chapter's description. Elder Futhark lacks the x and the ch sound. You must decide whether you want a phonetic translation or a letter-for-letter translation. Some of you may need to go to the Anglo-Saxon 33 letter alphabet for more phoneme options (but that is another book!)

The second issue became more problematic when the book gained popularity outside what I believed to be the initial audience. The runes come from Norwegian, Icelandic, German and Anglo-Saxon poems and the names each respective language uses for the runes is different, with a slightly different spelling, rhythm, and sound. When I sing or call the runes in rhythm, I often choose from these different pronunciations based on the sound and meter I am trying to create. One example is with the names Gifu and Gebo - they both mean Gift and Relationship, but one is Norwegian and the other Icelandic. I usually choose Gifu to sing as the vowels are more elegant and the consonant is less cumbersome. When I asked David which pronunciations to use for the first edition, he said just use the ones I like the best. This ultimately proved confusing and even off-putting for some readers who had either not studied other books or who desired academic consistency. We ultimately resolved the issue by using the proto-Germanic names for consistency in the second edition.

The third issue required a complete re-write of the divination section. Initially, I included the divination section only under duress. The runes are not like the tarot or other cultural tools that "tell the future." Old German and Old Norse did not have a future tense! The only thing certain is the past, that which is, historical precedence which may set the stage for the future but doesn't necessarily predict it. True, the later Sagas imply that there is a certainty of wyrd or destiny that is written and unable to be fought, but the later Sagas are also post-Christian and are understood in a different context. A clear discussion of wyrd, öorlog, the Norns, and the Nordic mindset have become more important for me to share in this book given the large number of people using the book and the iPhone application. I also mention using runes in healing, toning and creating "script" or "bind runes".

Minneapolis, 2016

About the Aettir (Ættir)

The 24 runes of the Elder Futhark are generally divided into three sets of eight runes each. Aett means clan or family in Old Norse. People related by blood, marriage, or adoption/oath would sit together in aettir (plural) at the annual gathering called Thing where legal disputes were settled. Since aett is pronounced "eight" and there are eight runes in each aett, folk etymology equates aett with eight.

While the oldest known inscription of the 24 runes on the Kylver stone in Gotland (400 AD) puts them in a long string, there are good reasons to divide them into three aettir. Breaking them up makes it easier to memorize and remember them. Adding a "head of the household" such as Freya/Freyr for the first aett, helps deepen the meaning and message of the particular clan of runes. Each aett becomes a story onto itself. Other writers have intuited this and have written their own versions of the stories of these aetts. As mentioned before, the runes are about relationships - a secret conversation and a listener. They are in relationship to their nature energies and to one another. It is natural to see groups of similarities and relationships that tell different parts of the story of the Northlands.

For me, the first aett is all about the balance between the landed farmer and the ranging herder, the giants and the gods, knowing and experiencing, relationships and joy. The second aett describes the world tree from the roots in fire and ice, to the middle farm/earth, to the sun that tops the tree. The third aett contains the names of god/goddess pairings, divine gifts to humanity, and the inheritance of these gifts and their responsibilities. I encourage you to read and explore for yourself the lessons of the aettir.

Finally, the aettir set up a numerological system within the alphabetic system that was used in communication and in esoteric work. In one system, the first number indicates the aett and the second number is the letter within the aett. So 1:3 = Thurisaz, 2:1 = Hagalaz, and 3:5 = Laguz. There are other applications which can be made by those of esoteric interest in numerology.

Freya/Freyr's Aett

"Hugging Gebo," Mississippi River Rune Walk, Kari Tauring
March 2016

Everything about runes and Norse Tradition is based on Gebo/Gifu, relationships, voluntary reciprocity, giving and receiving in balance. Nature is excellent at it, if only we will participate. My grandfather practiced reciprocity with Nature in his farming.

1. Fehu

Fehu, Fe: the phoneme F - domesticated cow and other animals, landed wealth, gold. The first rune in the alphabet. The shape of Fehu begins with Isa, the straight line, Ice (the rune of slow growth and contemplation). Then come two lines looking up to the right, like a modern day F with the lines raised upwards instead of extending perpendicularly. It reminds me of cow horns looking up to the sky.

The cow is the first gendered being to come into existence in Norse myth. Audhumbla, whose milk nourished the hermaphrodite giant Ymir, was said to have come from the stars. Our galaxy, the Milky Way, is named for the concept of milk flowing from the teats of Audhumbla. In all of the Indo-European alphabets from Egyptian hieroglyphs to the Roman letter A, the first letter means ox or cow. The advent of domestication coincides with the first alphabets, the flourishing of art, and an increase in population.

Who put the F in Futhark? Freya, Queen of the Vanir did! The first row of eight runes is often called Freya's Aett, and her twin brother, Freyr is implied within. Their names translate to Lady and Lord. These twin deities of the Vanir, the agricultural and herding deities who came before the Aesir to the Northlands, are the children of Njord, god of the shoreline and Nerthus, goddess of the earth. The people who worshipped them were landed, settled herders and famers who buried their dead in matrilineal graves. The accumulation of wealth that comes with being a settled culture extends the meaning of Fehu to gold, a metal precious to Freya.

The first domestic cows, sheep, and goats arrived up North during the Nordic Bronze Age (1700 - 500 BCE), brought out of Northern Iran in migrating waves. Scandinavia was warmer during that time, more Mediterranean. Limes and grapes grew in Denmark and southern Sweden and Norway and the reindeer continued to move north, out of the heat. Some of the traditional reindeer herders, the Sami, moved with them. Some of the original peoples stayed and intermingled with the new culture. And, I suspect, that the new culture pushed original inhabitants further north and off of the fertile land left by the Ice Age. Rock art and grave finds from the period proclaim shipping, hunting, and herding as major activities. Giant bronze lurs or blowing horns in pairs (left and right) and figurines showing dancing and ritual activity indicate a rich cultural life. The deities were most often shown in god/goddess pairings, copulating or otherwise creating fertility over their land.

My "home town" of Underdal on the Sognefjord is still most well known for their gjeitost, a carmel brown goat cheese. In a recent archeological excavation, they have found dairies of the same design used today dating to the Bronze Age. Remnants of gjeitost within prove a nearly 4,000 year unbroken tradition in this valley. That they continue to make a living in this way is the ultimate in Fehu.

Cows and goats were connected to women. Even the Immigrants from Norway were shocked to find that in America, men milked cows. Milking and churning were magical processes. Women's work was transformative, changing one thing into another, and magically potent. We know this because charms and songs for churning and other women's work were banned in church laws of the 1600's. In folk stories, it was Freya's women the Huldra, beautiful, alluring and magical women with cows' tails who taught human women how to keep cows, breed them, herd them, and how to churn milk and make butter, cheese, and skyr (like yogurt). They taught human women to keep clean houses and human men were attracted to them. In fact, they were highly sexual creatures and often compelled human men into the woods or under the hills from whence the men might never return (not unlike their mistress, Freya). Huldu (male of the Huldre) and Tomte or Nisse would often live in a farmhouse barn or out building. They helped with chores and were rewarded with food the farmers would leave out for them at night and on astronomically important days such as Winter and Summer Solstices.

The climate became wetter and colder at the end of the Bronze Age and by 400 AD when the first complete set of Elder Futhark runes was written (at least from what we have found so far), life had become much more difficult. Fehu, herding, milk production and farming takes on new shades of meaning in colder climates. Cheese may be the only thing that saves you from starvation during the long cold winter.

Today people think Fehu means wealth, and they write it on a pendant in hopes of accumulating money. Not so easy! Domesticated cows are a lot of work. They must be fed, watered and milked two times a day (at the same time) every day. You also need to store up hay for their winter fodder, and you have to help them birth their calves. You really have to be on it! My Norwegian ancestors had to do all this on a 45 degree slope. If you were lucky enough to have land and fortunate enough to own cows, the daily and nightly diligence of keeping them alive and productive was more than full time work, not unlike mothering. And, as with mothering, there is a deep bond and relationship between the cow and the human. Special songs to the cows (kulokk in Norwegian, kulning in Swedish) are still sung in the hills of Scandinavia and Finnish cow charms still exist on Minnesota's Iron Range.

In her book, "Cattle, an Informal Social History," Laurie Winn Carlson describes the intricate social relationship of cows and humans from Ice Age cave paintings in Spain and France to the modern era. Commoditizing cows, milk, cheese and butter has destroyed our relationship with this gentle and ever-giving animal. What was once sacred and nourishing is now commercial and unhealthy. Lactose intolerance is on the rise even in Northern European populations for whom milk consumption was salvation. Modern people's disconnection from the earth our food is grown in and the animals whose products we take for granted is Fehu reversed.

What does such a rune mean for the modern human? Sure, write this rune on your checkbook and savings account statements to remind yourself to keep careful track of what you are putting in, what you are taking out, and the quality of your investments. At the first writing of this book I was putting together my tax paperwork, looking at the past year trying to assess which jobs were consistently fruitful. Not just what created good income for me, but how was that income created? Is what I do to create income nourishing me spiritually, honoring the earth, honoring Freya and Freyr? The shift of meaning from domestic animals to gold is significant. As the Norwegian rune poem (circa 1200 ACE) laments, "Wealth is a source of discord among kinsmen." This discord has its root in the modern disconnect of money and life sustenance. Moderns are no longer connected to the food they eat, the water they drink or the air they breathe. To draw the rune Fehu means we should pay attention to the source of our nourishment and work to maintain a relationship to our food, water, air and soil.

Fehu is a rune of careful husbandry, diligence, cleverness, and hard work. Sometimes we are in the position of cowherd, and sometimes this rune represents our own selves as the cow. Sometimes we are helpless and look heavenward for help in meeting our needs. If this is the case, we should know that it's ok to be cared for. The cow, well-nurtured, creates an abundance of milk that can sustain the tribe even in the darkest of winters. So even as the cow, our work benefits others. Reversals of this rune simply mean that more attention and diligence should be paid to your finances and what is generating them. Are you investing in things that are sustainable and holy/hael/healthy? As a rune of the "lower chakra," sexuality, abundance, and grounding, is your job/income coming from and feeding your source or keeping you out of the loop of relationship to your source?

2. Uruz

Uruz: the phoneme u - the wild ox, aurochs. The second rune in the alphabet after Fehu, the domestic cow, and before Thurisaz, the rune which represents the Giants, Uruz is the wild cattle of the North, the predecessor to the domestic cow. It has been called the wild bison, synonymous to the wisent, but these are truly separate species. I call Uruz a lower chakra rune. In the Eastern system of energy where seven energy centers relate to points on our spines, the lower chakras are dark, red, and fiery and connected to sexuality, willfulness, and basic needs. Uruz speaks to these qualities. Ur means primal and is the root of the name Urd, the first of the Norns who keeps the well of primal waters called Urdarbrunnr.

Many consider Uruz to be a fire rune, and it is an ancient symbol. If you point your thumb and pointer finger towards earth they make the shape of Uruz. If you bend at the waist to touch your toes, your body creates this symbol. The shape is like the horns of the aurochs pointing to the ground. The aurochs are the ancestor of domesticated cows and roamed the hills and plains of Africa, Asia and Europe. They were an important source of sustenance and a subject of much cave art, similar to the Bison in North America. It would seem that Uruz should come before Fehu, chronologically. And these two runes describe the tension-filled relationship between the "Farmer and the Cowboy" that still exists in the American West.

Landed settlers and ranging herders are two completely different lifestyles, value systems, mindsets and cosmologies, different even in the way days, weeks, and seasons are marked and observed. This tension exists between the Sami reindeer herders and those who would build fences in the far north. The Elder Futhark tells the story of clashing cultures and their deities, and suggests ways of balancing them.

Uruz is a "hunter's rune." It was a group effort to take down the aurochs, and warrior hunters often came close to death in the process. What a thrill! It required courage, commitment, passion, and a strong will, other energies of this rune. This rune tells us to coil our energy, and feed and store it as we lie in wait for just the right moment to spring into action. If we panic in a fear of lack, we may spring on prey that is not sufficient to feed the whole family. Then when the right one comes along, we are spent. An equally important lesson is that the aurochs were hunted to extinction by "modern men." The last aurochs died in Poland in 1627. Too much fire in the belly can be consuming. Consequences can be tragic if this energy stays too long or is used too often.

If you have seen deer or horses running freely over the fields, you sense their beauty, grace, and freedom. Uruz is also about those qualities. It can help artists with their creative fire. It can help lovers with their lower chakra connections. It can help parents understand their toddlers and teenagers. Toddlers and teenagers share the common psychological state, "push me, pull you." They cling to the "feed me, love me, do for me" of Fehu, the domestic cow, while exploring the independence, freedom and passion of Uruz, the creator ox. Where Fehu is willing, Uruz is will*ful*. Fehu willingly submits to the attendance of the Mother while Uruz bucks willfully against it and may charge out of the house and slam the door. There are times in our lives when we need the fire of willfulness to draw boundaries, to make the final push to finish a project, or to create art. The balance of these energies is in Thorn.

In the story of Audhumla at the beginning of creation, Audhumla ranged over the salty brine around Ganungagap, the gaping void. Her udders dispensed the rivers of milk that fed the giant Ymir from whose sweat and body came the other giants. She licked the salty ice of the cosmos and uncovered a man, Buri, who had a son named Bor. Bor married the giant Bestla and they had three sons, Wod, Wili, and We (Odin, Vili and Ve, whose names mean Spirit, Will, and Holiness). The cow is at the center of many mythologies that came out of the Indus Valley. There is a deep and great respect for the cow, domestic or wild, in many cultures around the world. Uruz takes us to the beginning of time, the formation of the Milky Way, and calls us into deep respect for the essence of creation.

Uruz reversed generally indicates that one's life is not being lived passionately and that changes need to be made. For a time, it is fine to bear down and work without passion, but eventually that can douse the fire in the belly. Humans need to love their jobs, their work, their daily lives. I find American culture preaches tolerance for oppressive, "dead end," passionless lives. It helps marketing and sales if people are unhappy, oppressed, and dispassionate. It's a lot harder to sell things to people who are happy and fulfilled. Individuals need more Uruz, more passion for what they are doing in the world and the connection of Fehu to what they are producing. Fehu in terms of resources must be available to all, as our basic domestic needs must be met first if we are to find the bravery for individual passions.

American culture, as pictured in television, advertisements, and other media however, needs less Uruz. An excess of this rune can lead to self-indulgence, narcissism, and over consumption. The Norwegian rune poem says Uruz is dross - "Dross comes from bad iron; the reindeer often races over the frozen snow." As with Fehu turning from relationship with cows to gold, Uruz turns from the aurochs to the poison from iron production. Again, we moderns can take the warning that disconnecting from the energy and relationship of the natural world poisons our water, soil, and life itself. There is a longing feeling in the second line, as reindeer race over the frozen snow, reminding us of our more basic, pure, and connected way of being in the world.

Uruz is the rune that inspires, but not necessarily the rune that manifests or completes. It is significant that Uruz is followed by Thurisaz, as Thurisaz presents the potential of discernment and careful decision making.

3. Thurisaz

Thurisaz: the phoneme th - the rune of Thurses, Jotuns, giants, the elementals, also called Thorn. As we grow through the Futhark from the docile domestic cow to the wild ox, Thurisaz confronts us with our first opportunity to choose. It represents the dawning of our conscience and ability to discern right from wrong. In human brain evolution, this rune represents the moment, some four million years ago, when the cerebrum evolved, allowing us to replace purely instinctive actions with thoughtful and considered actions.

In the Norse myth of creation, Ymir, the hermaphrodite giant whose name means scream or howling groan, was a source of unconscious creation. Giants, dwarves, and all manner of beings were springing from her/his armpits, legs, and forming from sweat and vibration as she/he sucked at the teats of Audumbla the cosmic cow. Thurses (giants) of fire, ices, rocks and other elements were slaves to instinct and primitive emotional responses. The three sons of Bor and Bestla, Odin, Vili and Ve (Spirit, Will and Holiness), carved up the body of Ymir to create the world as we know it. This creation can be viewed as spirit, will and holiness ordering and organizing the primal sound into the music of the spheres.

In the Norwegian and Icelandic rune poems, Thurs is called the torture of women. Gjalp and Greip (listed as two of Heimdall's nine mothers) were said to guard the river Vimur. When Thor forced his way across the river, Gjalp straddled it and began to fill it with her rushing waters in order to drown the trespasser. Many scholars interpret the Vimur as the river of menses and connect the Thurs rune to women's moon time. It is certainly the most powerful, uncontrollable bodily fluid humanity has to offer and is the heart of many women's magical traditions. Thor pressed his way across this river by throwing a boulder into Gjalp's yoni. He eventually broke the backs of Gjalp and her sister Greip.

If Fehu is our baby stage and Uruz is our "terrible twos" then Thurisaz is the moment when we begin to use our reason. Anyone who works with children knows when reason is being engaged. When it is not, the sound of frustration, confusion, and willfulness is like Ymir. As we learn to tame our Thurse-like nature, we are able to give words to our emotions rather than allow our emotions to co-opt our actions.

Thurisaz has been equated with Thor, the son of Odin and Jord (Spirit and Earth) both because he defended Midgard against too many giants (ice giants in Winter and fire giants in Summer, and also because Thor himself had to go through stages of growth as he fought against the Thurses. The ultimate challenge for him and his major rite of passage into maturity as a god is told in the *Thrymskveda* or the Lay of Thrym. His hammer is stolen by the giant Thrym. Thor must dress up as Freya in bridal garments and remain calm and quiet at the bridal feast until Thrym calls for the hammer to be placed on his "bride's" lap. Only then can Thor re-claim his power.

Thor's hammer Mjolnir becomes the gavel that sounds after judgment is made. The mature Thor, the hammer wielder, presided over just causes and righteous decision making, sitting in council with the Norns at the well of Urd. Thor was most beloved of the Scandinavians. He was the working man's god. The symbol of his hammer was found in mints alongside the new Christian cross which, at the time, was depicted as two lines of equal length bound at the middle - the rune Gifu (balance of giving and receiving). The hammer symbol is found today in jewelry shops everywhere and is worn by both dedicants to the old religion and by those simply wishing to connect with their ancient heritage.

Thorn's shape is Isa, the ice rune, drawn along the mouth of Kenaz reversed. This suggests that we have enough choices in front of us and it is time to strike a path, to choose one way and go. Thorn suggests that we may seek aid in making the right decisions at this time, and that we are assured of support from the gods. There is a kind of poise in Thorn. The shape reminds me of stork legs, or my own legs when I rest one upon the other in a V shape like this rune. It asks us to take a moment of contemplation and evaluation, and then to strike out. The road will be clearly marked if we keep in mind what are good choices for us and what are not good choices. Thorn demands discernment.

The shape of Thorn also reminds me of an ax, a tool that benefits my life every day since my family heats our home primarily with wood. Our ancestors would have relied on this tool for their very lives. Remember, the worst injuries come from a dull blade. The sharpest ax is the best ax, and decisiveness and commitment to the cut is imperative in safety and effectiveness. This same understanding translates metaphorically to the decisions we make in our lives. Sharp, clear, simple and committed are the qualities we can evoke with the Thorn rune.

When we draw this rune, it means we face a choice. Sometimes this choice may seem blurry and confusing. One way to clarify things is to make an age-old list of pros and cons. Sometimes Thorn wants us to understand the concept of Universal Law or "Crow's Law" in Native American tradition. In Scandinavia, Universal law is known as *öorlog*, the fabric of individual destiny. The Norns take care of each person's *öorlog*, and Thor dispenses justice accordingly. The law of the Universe supersedes human law. Sometimes Universal Law and human law don't match up. But we must always yield to Universal Law. The choices we make each day send out waves to the rest of the world, which are represented in the next rune, Ansuz.

Thorn calls up the destructive nature of the Giants in the rune poem. The first life in the Universe was the Giant Ymir. It was from Ymir's sweat that Odin's parents were born. And Odin and his brothers killed their grandfather, creating the nine worlds from his body. This is the sort of creation from destruction that every mythological system describes in one way or another. The Frost Giants become the doom of gods and men at Ragnorok (the Nordic Armageddon) when they come to avenge Ymir. Worlds end and collapse, the world tree burns, but new worlds are born. This too is Crow's Law, the law of the Universe, the law of contraction and expansion, of death and rebirth. It is up to us to see where we and our choices fall in the cycle of life. Thorn helps us to make the decisions that benefit our highest path.

4. Ansuz

Ansuz, Oss, Os: the phoneme a (ah) - mouth of the river, the mouth of god, language and what comes out of my own mouth. I know this rune! It's the second letter of my name, A. You find Ansuz when you look at the trees. The shape is Isa, the straight line, then a line like half an arrow tip from the top (North), slanting to the Southeast. Then there is another line beneath. The shape is opposite Fehu (the cow's) shape. While the cow's horns are raised to the sky in expectation, Ansuz's horns are bent downwards in meditation or supplication. Ansuz has a prayerful look. But it is an active contemplation, an ever flowing and changing understanding, like a river.

The three roots of the world tree grow up out of the three wellsprings of the nine worlds, Urdsbrunner, Mimirsbrunner, and Hvergalmir. Hvergalmir is the headwater of the rivers. The rivers flow and empty into greater bodies of water at their mouths. In Tai Chi, they say the bubbling wells are at the bottoms of our feet, and we need to keep our feet open to receive that energy. That too is the power of Ansuz. We can walk quietly in power, drawing up energy from the bubbling wells to create a flow of chi through our bodies and out into the universe. In Nordic terminology, align your body with the World Tree, sink your roots into the three wells, and breathe your truth.

Sometimes Ansuz reminds me to do this work. As I align with the tree, my mind quiets, my bodies align, my energy flows with the energy of creation and I become one with my world. Then I can touch the source of my being and find that the source of my being is one with the divine!

The river has always been a place of worship. As the locations of ancient sacrifices to Christian baptisms, the waters of the river hold power. Rivers are a major source for food and water essential to life, cleanliness, transportation, commerce and trade. Communities tend to emerge alongside rivers. Cleanliness of our rivers is key to the health and survival of our whole ecosystem. The Ganges in India is considered to be so sacred that no matter how polluted it has become, people drink of it every day. It is considered to be the Mother of India, flowing out of a sacred mountain. A river may spring up from deep in the earth like the Mississippi, flowing and swelling, carrying tributaries until it empties into the Gulf of Mexico and out into the Ocean. I live by the Mississippi River in Minneapolis. The water is dirty and polluted, far from drinkable. What finally empties out of the mouth in the Gulf of Mexico does not contribute to the greater good and health of the planet and her creatures. But the only way to clean the river is at its source, by removing pollutants and polluters. Only then can you work your way down. It is the same with this rune, find the wellspring, follow it, and then you will know what comes out of its mouth.

When you draw Ansuz, first ask: what is the source of the issue, question, or creative problem I face? Then ask: is what I spew out of the mouth of *my* river in alignment with my source? Sometimes our emotions are a composite of many other emotions whose source is far removed from the trigger of the current emotional state. Water is emotions, and Ansuz is a water rune like Laguz (lake), Isa (ice), and Hagal (hail.) It asks us to find the source of our being and thereby the path of our life's journey. The Norwegian rune poem calls it an estuary, a holding place for all the rivers to feed into it, a place to contemplate and integrate diversity before opening up into the sea.

The rune that comes before Ansuz is Thorn, the decision maker, which represents confrontation with our source. Then comes Ansuz, the contemplation of our choice and path. Next is Rad, the wheel, the journeyman's rune. If we have moved through the order of our runes wisely, we should be ready for that long journey of our life's work.

As the mouth of god, Ansuz suggests that individual truth and wisdom lies within a greater context of Universal or Divine Truth. How do these truths align and how do they spill out into and mix with the larger body of wisdom, the sea? Knowledge of the source of things is within your understanding. Many people believe Ansuz presages some advisement by persons older or wiser, and it's always good to look around for wise people who can guide you. It also asks you to pray, even in its visual aspect. Ultimately, each of us knows why we are here on earth at this time. Each of us knows "god's highest will and purpose for our lives," as my great uncle Al used to say. If we but still our Thorn-like questioning and bend our heads to listen, we will perceive the source of our being.

The Anglo-Saxon rune poem calls Ansuz language, or words. It asks us to listen and take care of the words we speak. The mouth is the breath's door, and our words create reality. This rune warns us to watch what we say and how we say it. As the late Masaru Emoto [www.masaru-emoto.net] wrote in his book about water crystals, our words effect how water crystals form and develop. Our aspirations affect reality in subtle and profound ways. In the New Testament book of John it says that in the beginning was the Word and the Word was God. God is a word. The name of God in the Old Testament is a word that must never be spoken or written. The Hopi creation story talks about Thought Woman who thinks the world into being.

In Norse tradition this rune is Odin whose name means Spirit and the inspired word. He and his brothers Will and Holiness combine to create humanity. They gave us the power to articulate, to use breath with will and purpose towards divine action. It's quantum physics in mythology! We create reality with our words. Language is what makes us human and divine at once. Language describes reality and creates it. Language has its source in thought. Humans think things into being too! Hypochondriacs create illness. Optimists create opportunities. Ansuz wants to know if your thoughts and words are clean, clear, and aligned. Are you creating a life from the source of your divinity, or are you creating a life out of projected fears?

5. Raido

Raido, Rad: phoneme r - riding, vehicle, journey, wheel, and cycles. Once we understand the source of our being from Ansuz, the mouth of god, we must take this understanding into the world and try it out. To me, Raido is the journeyman's rune. As a musician, this rune represents the lessons learned on the road. Once we have learned our instruments, it's time to sharpen our chops. This rune tests us. After this journey comes Kenaz, the understanding and controlled torch of our craft. This excellence can only come after we have "paid our dues" so to speak.

The rune poems talk about the journey being swift and a joy to the rider, but the horse toils and it is the worst thing for them. It seems easy to warriors who stay indoors and relies on a sturdy horse. I have been doing much traveling and teaching in the past few years. The journey started out joyfully, but every band has an on-the-road lament about missing home, family, and friends. It becomes a toil fairly quickly when the glamor wears off.

Raido is the journey and even more, the vehicle we travel in - the band van, the road, the gas stations and auto shops...the air plane, the boat or train. Raido is a traveler's rune where the joy in the journey counts on all vehicles and vehicle assistants to be working properly.

We can carry more things and people across the land if we have a wagon or chariot. Yet, we are bound to using roadways where we are subject to mud, landslides, felled trees, and bandits who prey on our slow pace. And if we should break a wheel, we may find ourselves not moving at all. Raido may suggest we ask ourselves, how prepared are we for this journey? How certain are we that we need to take it? How dedicated are we? What vehicle have we chosen to carry our life's work?

Raido asks that we examine the relationship to the vehicle of movement we have chosen. In a business setting, this rune asks you to pay attention to the vehicle of advertising or product distribution. The vehicle for getting our message across, or the vehicle for collecting payment on our invoices are all part of this rune. We may think of other "delivery systems" in our lives, especially after Ansuz. How we deliver bad news can make a difference emotionally on how well we and others "move through" the process of grief, for example. Raido may be asking you to look at your word choices and emotional maturity in this case.

Raido as vehicle also means the physical body which is the vehicle for the soul. One thing we must be careful of while on our journey is how our body, our ultimate vehicle, is faring. Getting enough sleep, water, and healthful food while traveling can be nearly impossible. But without our bodies, our souls would flee! There has to be a balance. This rune may be asking you whether you need a massage or chiropractic adjustment or an herbal laxative. Is your body worn out, stuck, or out of condition?

Dreams are another vehicle for our spiritual life. It's possible that this rune is asking you to look into your dream time to acquire awake time information. In Norse tradition, dreams are a vehicle for our ancestors to visit us, to give us vital information and support. When an ancestor comes to you in a dream, pay attention, write it down, and work with it. This is truly a wonderful vehicle for getting us from A to B spiritually, emotionally, and otherwise.

Raido is a rune of change as a vehicle implies movement. We can't make the shift completely on our own and are once removed from the source of movement. We are drawn forward by the gods, by circumstances, and by our own dedication to learning the lessons of the journey. Taking my music out into other communities was an important and necessary step to finding my true voice. There is nothing like performing in front of strangers from different parts of the country. The feedback is powerful.

Raido implies relationships. Our relationship to the people we travel with, the people we meet on the way, the chance encounters and the lasting friendships are all important as we struggle to find out who we are and what our life's purpose is. Everyone we meet is a mirror for us. What do we like about other people, and what do we not? Do we have good boundaries with strangers? Do others have good boundaries with us? How does the feeling of lonely exhaustion change what we are willing to experience with others? If we feel alone on the journey, who can we turn to for comfort in a safe and healthy way?

So what is your journey? Going off to college, starting a new job, moving to another town or country, moving in with your partner, starting a family and shifting your career focus are all beginning points of journeys. And what is the vehicle you are choosing to get there? This rune asks you: How will you travel? Who will you meet and how will you treat them? How will you take care of yourself while on this journey? In this we can learn our lessons to make our "Aha!" with, the next rune, Kenaz a very powerful thing indeed.

6. Kenaz

Kenaz, Kaunan, Ken: phoneme k - torch, ulcer, to know or understand. This rune begins my name, Kari. It means that nothing is beyond my ken, my ability to understand, and I am never lacking in good ideas. The trick is to pursue only one idea at a time and be patient in manifesting it!

After Raido brings us through our journeyman's time, the *ah ha!* goes off. That's Kenaz. It's when we recognize ourselves and become aware of our understanding. In the Greek myth of Psyche and Eros, the god is afraid that if she sees his beauty in the light, her love will change from pure and innocent to that kind kindled by the eyes rather than the heart. But the moment she lights a candle and looks at the god's face, her pure love deepens. His mother, seeing purity of love even through the glamor of deity, lifts her up to goddess standing. Kenaz is the candle in the dark that lets us understand our relationship to the divine.

In the Hebrew book of Genesis, Kenaz is the moment Eve eats the forbidden fruit, suddenly possessing the knowledge of good and evil. As the angels said, "they will be like us if they eat of that tree." Suddenly Eve understands herself as an individual with free will, just as the angels have. Her life is forever changed. Kenaz, knowledge and understanding change us.

Kenaz is a fire rune. It is the light bulb that goes off and a fire that humans can use. In Celtic tradition it is the triple fire of goddess/saint Brigid: the fire of hearth and healing, the fire of the smith and crafting, and the inspirational fire of poetry. Oral poetry was the essence of Celtic and Nordic culture. Long ballads about gods, heroes, and extraordinary circumstances abound in Celtic music and storytelling.

The oral poetic tradition in the Nordic lands was written down by anonymous authors during the post-Viking and post-Christian era in Iceland. The Poetic Edda (Edda means grandmother) relies on alliteration, rhythm, and *kennings*, words that describe the subject in complex and symbolic manner. For example, instead of saying, "I will sail this ship," the skald might say "I will ride this wind horse." Using Kennings cleverly and accurately says two things about you as a speaker. You are a good listener and observer of your surroundings. You perceive the subtleties of people, places, and things. You are able to use language to describe the intricacies of what you are observing. These qualities are highly valued by humans all over the world. Snorri Sturluson's later Icelandic Prose Edda is dedicated to helping the Nordic skald learn the kennings of all the beings in the nine worlds.

The Kenaz rune looks like the lesser than or greater than symbol, or a V on its side with the gaping mouth opening to the right. It conjures up an image of opening out. Information once closed off from me is now open to me to for understanding. If I draw Kenaz the other direction, it suggests that my ideas are crystallizing into a discernible point. It might also mean that it's time to hone my choices and focus on one or two projects, seeing them through to their ends.

Having ideas is one thing. Kenaz suggests that you are also able to manifest them, to take the fire of understanding, control it, and use it for your own means. Another lesson in Kenaz is the timing of your *ah ha*, the hatching of your plan, and knowing you now have the available resources to do what you must do. But remember this, just because something is a good idea does not mean you have to manifest it! If I tried to manifest every good idea I had I would be well worn out.

The Icelandic rune poem says that Kenaz is like an ulcer, or an eruption from within, that bursts forth. In Louise Hay's [www.louisehay.com] book about the emotional causes of disease, ulcers develop from fear that there is not enough time to implement our ideas. A sense of necessity and urgency comes with Kenaz. It compels us to action. We are not to stand in the enlightenment of knowing and do nothing with that knowledge. At the same time, we must only take on what we are capable of completing.

I often call Kenaz the rune of the crafters, artisans, poets, and people who share their inspiration with others. Sharing moves us to Gebo, Gifu, the gift rune which represents our impulse to share what we have learned and created from our knowing. To create things to give to others, but this has to be in balance with receiving or Gifu is out of balance and the result is the need rune, Naudiz. Remember in the manifestation of your great *ah ha* that it may take others to help implement your ideas and you must be receptive to their methods of helping you. You cannot and should not control or micro-manage everything. Sometimes the vision must change as it manifests. If you don't stay flexible with your flame, ulcers will certainly result!

7. Gebo

Gebo, Gifu: the phoneme g - gifting relationships. This rune looks like an X and carries the sound for G. The X shape is seen in the shapes of five of the 24 runes. It is one of the most common shapes in the architecture of stav churches and other buildings. Gebo is two stavs of equal length, leaning into one another and bound in the middle, a sturdy structure, to be sure, and one that suggests humans in relationship. It is the seventh rune in the alphabet, coming after Kenaz, the rune of knowing and *a ha!* discoveries, and before Wunjo the rune of blissful joy. After making an *a ha* discovery, we put that knowledge to use and the result manifests itself in gifts to the community and the relationships born from gifting. New inventions, new understanding, new songs and poems are nothing without an audience. And to give in this way produces joy, the final rune of this aett.

In Norse tradition, everything is about relationships and Gebo is one of the most important runes we have. Our relationship to our environment, our ancestors, our community, our deities, are what defines us in Norse tradition. People identified themselves by their relationship to where they live, taking the name of the farm (Engen or Rudigard), the land (Nedberg or Nykkreim), who their fathers or mothers were (as in Gudridsdottir or Erikson) or by their relationship to deity (Freydis or Wodansgothi). Name and lineage are extremely important. Even weapons and tools have names and histories with the user and most likely the user's ancestors who passed the tools down.

Relationship even describes indigenous healing methods of Nordic peoples. Being able to give the name and lineage of an illness is to be in relationship to it whereby the healer can then make deals with it, request it to leave the body of the inflicted and offer it another more suitable home. There is a Finnish charm against frostbite that I love which describes this relationship very well. It was still known in Minnesota in the late 1930's. It addresses the source of frostbite, "Cold, son of the puff of wind, don't freeze my hands...freeze instead the water willows..."

A gift requires a receiver and creates relationship, *self to self* or *self to other*, there is always an "I and thou" in giving. Relationships are what the runes are all about. Relationships are what life on Earth is all about. We are nothing on our own. The fastest way to destroy something is to ignore it. Ignored, we die. On the other hand, the fastest way to grow something is to pay attention to it, nurture it and love it. Being in relationships with others, and defining, nurturing and building those relationships are the greatest survival skill humans possess. In social anthropology this is called the biochemical feedback mechanism. The chemical reactions that occur when we nurture functional relationships encourage us to continue those relationships. We build social systems that enhance the sense of well-being that comes from the chemicals released by these positive interactions. These systems are interconnected and interdependent. Familial, tribal, educational, religious and governmental systems work together to preserve humankind.

Today's culture often separates these systems and creates structures or institutions that do not see all parts of the culture as a whole unit. These structures do not create the same chemical reactions that systems create. They tend towards isolating individuals from community groups, and hierarchies take the place of communities. Instead of generating the feeling of empowerment through belonging, individuals feel isolated and powerless. The ultimate gift we can give is the simple acknowledgment of existence. "I see you. I acknowledge you." This is something we must, in many ways, re-learn as a culture.

Nothing kills a plant, animal, person, idea...faster than ignoring it. So even the simple act of eye contact and a brief nod of the head is Gebo!

It is amazing to me in my Nordic Roots dance research and practice how many little Gebos are made in dance postures. In a community circle dance we hold the left palm up to receive the palm of the person next to us and the right palm down to be received. We cross our thumbs in little Gebos to lock ourselves together and begin to move in a wave of connection and balance in giving and receiving. When dancing in pairs, we can face one another and make Gebo by grasping left hand to left and right to right, spinning in a vortex of stable relationship.

Gebo is about giving and receiving in balance. Remember, both stavs of this rune are of equal length and bound at the middle. If you are giving more than you are receiving or receiving more than you are giving, you get Naudiz, the need fire rune; one sturdy stav and one spindly one sitting askew at the top of the sturdy one. You must be Gebo within yourself or you can't be Gebo with anyone else. In the Havamal (second poem in the Eddas) Odin is giving advice about relationships and gifting. One of the verses translates to "a gift demands a gift" which some modern Heathens have taken to the extreme in an almost "gifting war" kind of behavior, "one upping" each other in gift giving. Among close friends this can be a lot of fun, especially if you see one another only a few times each year. As a cultural attitude, however, this could put a strain on resources as well as the emotional value of giving without the thought or receiving anything back or receiving without the anxiety of "now what can I do to give back." This puts Gebo into a Naudiz position.

In Beowulf and other old stories, a kenning for a war chieftain is "ring giver" or "gold hater." In a warring society where loyalty of the soldiers needed to be purchased, leaders would be generous with their wealth. This gifting was done ritually in Horn Ceremony and in front of the whole community. Often oaths were sworn with the gifting over the horn which connected everyone's öorlog to the same wyrd. Other serious oaths would be done over an oath ring. There was always a Law Speaker carefully recording who said what and who promised what so that if there were misunderstandings they could be brought up at Thing (yearly council) where grievances were settled, oaths renewed and sometimes marriages were performed.

As Norway began to regain independence as a nation after 400 years of being an underdeveloped colony of Denmark in the mid-1800's, the artists, poets, and political intelligentsia began to look for ways to define themselves as Norwegian. They went out to the farmers and crafters of the rural areas who they believed must have kept the essence of "Norwegian-ness" alive in the folk costumes, dialects, music and dance. Here they found a remarkable social principal among the farmers called "voluntary reciprocity" in the language of 19th Century Romanticism. The essence of Gebo/Gifu, an ancient concept indeed and the driving force of social and political life in Norway into modern times.

True community takes care of all members. Therefore, the smaller stavs (children and elderly) are placed in the center of the community, little Gebos. Surrounding them are the big stavs (Isa) who support them. This is the little Gebo in Mannaz, the rune of humanity, community - Manneheim. Another combination to make this rune is taking two Naudiz, two need fires together can create Mannaz. Isa and Naudiz begin the next aett. Gebo is the balance of the ingard (inside the farm enclosure) and utgard (the wild world beyond the fence). This balance is what keeps the community safe and prosperous, safe from outside attacks (by man or beast or troll) and prosperous by venturing out to hunt, fish and trade. There are good lessons for personal boundary setting with this concept of Gebo as the keeper of the ebb and flow from our innermost beings to the outside world. The staff carriers were the border walkers of ingard and utgard for the seen and unseen community, balancing their own Gebo on the edge of Mannaz.

Gebo asks us to look inside and outside ourselves to see how our relationships are doing. It asks us to be aware of the relationships that support us regarding the question at hand. Are we using our gifts and talents for the benefit of the whole community, our children, our mates? What is our reciprocal relationship to the others in our household, pets and plants included? The full meaning of this rune depends on the runes surrounding it in a question. If it is a yes and no question, the answer is always the positive. But Gebo asks us to evaluate our gifts and to give of ourselves, to evaluate our relationships and make certain that there is equality in giving and receiving, to be certain we are bound to one another. It is up to us to be sure these relationships are healthy and functional. This is the essence of Gebo.

8. Wunjo

Wunjo, Wynn: phoneme w or v - joy Wunjo represents joy, pure joy, the kind that comes from giving and receiving with the right balance of pride and humility, unconditionally and without ego. When we are so happy that tears come to our eyes it is because we feel thankful, because we have full awareness of the gifts bestowed upon us by others and the world. This is in contrast to thinking that source of our joy stems from our industry alone. Wunjo recognizes all aspects of success.

Wunjo is a straight line (Isa), with Kenaz reversed coming from the top to the middle. It looks like Thorn only the Kenaz is at the top rather than in the middle. With Thorn, our Ken or knowing turns in on our care and caution, creating two paths from which to choose. With Wunjo there is only one path. It is the right one, and that creates joy. It puts a spring in the step of one who is walking confidently in their pathway.

Scandinavia is a land of extremes. Total darkness in winter and total light in the summer helps create a psyche that is used to extremes. The kind of joy Wunjo speaks of is extreme bliss. Lack of sunlight and cold temperatures create a sorrow and depression called Seasonal Affective Disorder, or S.A.D., which causes us to mourn, sometimes to drink to excess or medicate ourselves in other ways. The depths of despair drills holes in our souls. The deeper the well of our sadness, the greater our capacity for joy. The extremes of the land create extremes in the culture. This is why Yuletide, the midwinter festival, lasts for upwards of two weeks in Scandinavia with specific rituals and foods for each day. Sun wheel-shaped breads colored with saffron, golden puddings, and honey mead are all part of the feasts in the dark days.

With so few days in the growing season and so many provisions to put up for the next long dark haul, summer is a frenzy of work. Midsummer is a time to travel when the roads and water ways are clear of ice and snow. It is a time to work hard all day and then play deep into the night. There are bonfires and picnics and parties and dances. In summertime the men go *viking*, and the women take the herds up to the summer farms. There is a joy in life, in being alive, in having made it through yet another grueling and unforgivably dark, hard winter. There is a lightness of being, a joy that is called Wunjo.

Wunjo is the last rune in the aett of Freya and Freyr. These Vanir deities are well known for their love of the physical pleasures. Wunjo comes from feeling comfortable in your skin, confident in your beliefs and the usefulness of your work. Joy comes from doing a good day's work, of knowing your path and walking it. It is the gift of the gods, and it fills our hearts so full that we may even come to tears. If this rune is reversed you are being asked to review your life. Is your daily routine out of alignment with your divine purpose? How can you fix this?

Joseph Campbell said, "Follow your bliss." Wunjo tells us the same. If we do not follow our bliss, our life's true path, we will remain unfulfilled. If we do follow our bliss, we increase our luck, strengthen our öorlog, and create strong wyrd in the community. It is sad to not be in love with our lives when it is possible for all of us. Follow Gebo into Wunjo for the next rune is the hailstorm.

Heimdal/Hela's Aett

"Jack Frost Runes", photo by Kari Tauring, Minneapolis Winter, 2015.

Finding runes in nature is easy if you know them well and develop a relationship with them, you will see them everywhere. In the leaf-less trees, in the ski trails...these were left on my wind shield for me one cold winter morning.

9. Hagal*az*

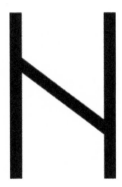

Hagalaz, Hagal: phoneme h - hail. In addition to Hel and Heimdal's Aett, I am also known to call this family the Norn's Aett because the first three runes in this family are primal force runes: hail, need fire and ice. This aett starts in the lower worlds of the cosmic tree and builds upwards to the Sun. According to the Voluspa, in the beginning of time, ice and fire came together in the Gaping Void. And from a particular combination of heat and cold in the atmosphere came hail. Hail is usually brief and often unexpected. It can cause devastation and death, yet both the Icelandic and Norwegian rune poems call it the "coldest of grain" – As we know from the story of Audumbla, ice holds the patterns of new life. Hail can destroy the old but that, in turn, makes way for the new.

Hail is an element of the creative force, primal and deep. Hela holds the cauldron of re-birth in the gaping void. She sends this essence in an updraft to the Heavens where Heimdal can watch and direct it. He has infused his divinity among humans from the lowest to the highest consciousness and being. As the Eddaic poem, Lay of Rig, tells us, Heimdal does not discriminate but engenders his divine essence among all humanity.

Hail is caused by a strong updraft in a storm system, the same updraft that causes thunderstorms. This can connect the rune to Thor as well. His powerful storms fertilize and waken the Earth. You often find damaging winds and tornadoes along with hail. So when you pull Hagalaz, the best idea is to duck and take cover for the duration of the storm. Then, once the storm has passed, assess the damage, take stock of what has been destroyed, repair what can be repaired, and say a prayer of thanks to the gods for what has been spared. Of course the hail storm rune follows Wunjo, the joy/bliss rune. Bliss has lifted us high, but it's time to come down off the mountain top to experience and mix with common mortals. The hail storm is like a reality check. The rune that follows is need.

Heimdal is the watcher of Bifrost the rainbow bridge and the ruler of the space between Midgard and the upper worlds. Hail and Ice are crystalline structures whose surfaces contain a myriad of rainbow bridges. Heimdal is the son of the nine mothers, giant women who turn the mill wheel that creates the elements of salt and earth. Heimdal was born through an up-swelling of the sea. He is the silent warrior who guards Bifrost, waiting for Loki and the Fire Giants to come and cause their destruction at Ragnarok. Our model for how to behave during a hailstorm is to stand still, be quiet, and wait. Like Heimdal, no matter how diligent we are, we still cannot stop the destruction, but we can blow the Gjallerhorn and warn others. And when the timing is right we can go out into the world to see what we can do, what lives we can save, what homes we can rebuild, and what we can recreate out of the debris.

Hel (or Hela) rules the land of the dead, Helheim. Her name means whole, healthy, and holy. Hela's face is half crone and half maiden, she is that mysterious fourth face of the Goddess, the death crone that begets the maiden aspect. We all know how a woman can go from maiden to mother and from mother to crone, but what about crone to maiden again? This is Hela's mystery. She is the "fourth Norn" in Disney's animated version of Sleeping Beauty. This fourth face was forgotten, it is too scary, to mysterious and uninvited to the birthing. Hence, the wrath of Hela. Beauty will be suspended forever as maiden, never moving through her cycles, through pricking her finger on a spindle, Hela will stop the wheel from turning. Wholeness remains un-achieved.

As the daughter of Loki the trickster, one can imagine that sudden bursts of hail might be Hela's way of shifting souls along. And, as I mentioned, facing the possibility of death in a hailstorm changes the way people conduct the rest of their lives. In this way, I also relate Hagalaz to the Norn Verthandi (Verdandi), the present moment. Nothing sobers us up faster to the moment's necessity better than a fierce natural phenomenon like a sudden hail storm. This rune reminds me to remain calm, sober and present and wait in an active state for need to show itself.

Remember, hail happens. It's not your fault, and there's nothing you can do to prevent it. As the serenity prayer says, fix what you can, leave alone what you can't fix and be wise enough to know the difference. Hail comes unexpectedly, and the difficulty of predicting it is the cause of most of the associated deaths. Another mistake that increases hail's destructive power is thinking we are immortal. Being willful in a hailstorm is a huge danger, and when I draw this rune I always try to think about areas in which I am being boastful or over confident as that is the area the storm is most likely to hit. I also look to my community for help, since during hardship, other people can help keep us alive.

Hail can be an extremely damaging force of nature, killing crops, breaking tree limbs, crushing skulls of livestock and humans. A friend of mine once got caught in a hailstorm in the Badlands of South Dakota. His truck was demolished, and the only thing between his head and the glass from his windshield was a South Dakota map he hid under. Experiences like this change us. We become more grateful for life, aware of what is really important, and sometimes it starts us on a new path in life. What comes after Hagalaz in the alphabet? Naudiz, the need fire, the rune that makes us evaluate our real and true needs. Nothing like a near death experience to point out what is a need and what is simple desire.

The good news is hail doesn't last long. A blizzard can go on for days, but the world's longest reported hailstorms have generally not lasted more than 30 minutes. One, in Alberta, Canada in 1991, with 4-inch hail, caused over $300 million dollars in damage to homes and property. Another in China in 1932 reportedly killed 200 people and injured thousands more.

Hagalaz is the rune of a clean slate and can even be used intentionally to clear our lives of things, people, and attitudes that are not helpful. It gives us the opportunity to start over and learn from it. There is a certain buzz or energy that one gets in the face of nature's fury. Use this energy to rebuild your life with stronger structures and heartier crops. A clear field, a blank canvas – destruction is the first step in creation as so many of the runes remind us. Use this rune and the energy it provides to create anew from the ashes. It's exhilarating to be granted a new beginning, but we have to wait for the destruction to pass. The learning of Hagalaz is patience while waiting out the storm, prayer, honest evaluation of what you have left to work with, and action again in the rebuilding of your life.

10. Naudiz

Naudiz, Neid: phoneme n - need and necessity, the need fire.
Naudiz is Gebo out of balance. Someone has too much and some
other, not enough. Someone is giving and not receiving. Someone is
receiving without giving. There is an imbalance. Things are not
whole, not hale, not healthy, not holy. It comes after Hagalaz has
brought us into the threshold. Need is always apparent after the
destruction of a storm. Then comes Isa, ice, the solidified waters of
öorlog, the core of the glacier telling us the whole Earth story. We are
placed in the state of need after the hailstorm and the evaluative head
space need puts us in is how we can "read" or make use of Isa. Isa and
Naudiz (ice and fire), the first two elements of the creation of the
cosmos, come together to create Hagalaz (hail).

To me, the Norn Urd is represented by the Ice core, reading the
history of the Earth and all öorlog. Verthandi is like Hagalaz, in the
threshold of becoming. Naudiz is, to me, the rune of Skuld, the Norn
who shows up at the time of our great need to guide us. The Norns are
called Naudigastir, Need's guests, compelled to appear twice in our
lives at the times of our greatest need, birth and death. In parts of
Norway they still set out a bowl of *nornargrøt* (norn porridge), a gift,
a Gebo, creating relationship between the Norns and the baby. It is
hoped that the Norns might weave a gentle web of wyrd for the child,
keeping her or him from desperate need in their lives.

Skuld's name is cognate to the words should and shild or debt. She reminds us of what we owe to our ancestors, to nature, and to the gods for our very existence. Think of it in terms of gardening. Once we have grown our crop and harvested it, we now must make amendments to the soil, energizing it again after the depletion of growth. This puts us back in Gebo with the Earth!

We owe honor and remembrance to our ancestors for our existence. We must also remember that which constricted them, caused them to need and perhaps caused needs to go unmet. These are the things that leave attachments or markers of stress in our DNA. These are things that once they are remembered and healed, can relieve us and our decedents from perpetual patterns of dysfunction based on unhealed Naudiz.

Skuld is first among Valkyries, the choice maidens who appear on the battlefields choosing who will live and who will die. Their duties include leading the souls of those who die in battle to either Odin or Freya's halls directly, avoiding the journey to Hela's hall, a journey the rest of us must take. Skuld sways the battle to come out the way it *should*. In the Voluspa, the seer remembers that the norns score or make marks, possibly runes. They write down the laws and choose all the lives, according to what should, by necessity, happen.

Naudiz is a fire rune along with Kenaz, the torch, controlled fire of understanding. Need is the creative fire, the mother of invention, and the community fire that keeps us all alive. Need feeds our ken and ken is the result of need. As the Norwegian rune poem says, "Constraint gives scant choice, a naked man is chilled by the frost." Naudiz asks us to sit down and draw up our lists of what is truly necessary to our lives and goals. What are our wants or desires? Who determines what we really need? List the influences in your life that tell you what your essence is. Clearing out the stuff we don't really need in turn makes room for our true needs to be fulfilled.

Need fire - In Minnesota, I continue in my family tradition of heating and cooking with a wood stove. Unlike my mother when she was growing up on the Wisconsin farm, I also have a really nice furnace I can rely on. I am not as close to the edge of Naudiz as she was growing up, or as her mother and grandmother before her, where in the middle of the night in the middle of the winter in the middle of the North if the fire in your wood stove died, so might you.

The Icelandic rune poem calls it "grief of the bond-maid and state of oppression and toilsome work." It often fell to children to gather, chop and carry wood. Attention to the fire requires diligence. In Lithuania there is a little red and black snake goddess called Aspelene who guards the corner behind the wood stove! In the afternoon when we are all out doing chores, we have to carefully bank the coals. When it's time to cook we stoke the fire. We rarely let the essence of the hearth go out. Nomadic Northerners learned to carry the embers from the winter camp to the spring camp. They knew which sticks and stones make the best sparks. Living in a subsistence family unit, everyone took part in keeping the Need Fire in Gebo.

Naudiz is Gebo out of balance. Look to Gebo for how to fix this. In community, we must take care of our children who are our future and our elders who are our past, and the fire, our central tool of survival. To manage this, we draw a circle around them and set up a system of protection. It is our physical, social, and spiritual duty. The old rune Naudiz was the center of the culture and the center of the individual's drive to improve the conditions of society. It is not just a social structure, but a true system, one that recognizes all parts as integral (see Manaz).

What is significant about the idea of Naudiz - the need fire - in today's society? Our culture has made our basic survival needs so cheap and easy to obtain that we have grown dependent on the grocery store and upon oil and gas to heat our homes. Children grow up not even knowing where their food originates - the cow gives milk, not the grocery store. This dependency exists so that we can be marketed to and told what our needs are. We are encouraged to live so far from the true need fire that we no longer know how to take care of ourselves, our children or the elderly that we are obligated to protect. We are fed soda pop, fast food, and things that cause disease. Then we are sold remedies for these diseases. Television isolates us from one another and the community. The real need fire makes us feel secure by our efforts, but also feeds our desire to strive, know, question, and invent.

Perhaps it is time for you to "get real." Spend a day and night without electricity or clean hot water pumped into your bath tub. Journal by candlelight. How does that feel? Bake your own bread. See how you can meet your basic needs without relying on others. Then think of your other needs besides the physical. Emotional security, being loved and loving others, creativity and spiritual expression are all needs. How are they being met? What do you need to change in your life in order to live more closely to the need fire? How about the children in your community? Do they have fire in their bellies? What about the elders on your block? Think, evaluate, and take action based on true need. The Anglo-Saxon rune poem sums it up beautifully - "Trouble is oppressive to the heart; yet often it proves a source of help and salvation to the children of men, to everyone who heeds it betimes."

11. Isa

Isa, Is: phoneme i - ice Isa is a simple straight line, running north to south. It is the "stop, look and listen" rune. The straight line is found everywhere in nature and is one of the oldest symbols. It represents humans, spines, trees, and staves. In 18 of the 24 runes, a straight vertical line plays part in the symbol's creation. In later Viking times, the 16 runes (Younger Futhark) used were created based on a single stav, so the shape of each one could be created with the body in runic postures. When we align our spines with the World Tree, we can also "grasp" the runes that come from its branches and roots. This is the posture of Isa, three roots and spine plumb. It is the stance we make when we begin to cross the frozen lake or an icy sidewalk. In Martial Arts it is called the Horse Riding Stance.

Isa depicts the essence of Nordic movement from dancing to skiing to walking on the frozen lake. The movement of the body in stav, plumb with the earth, straight backed with hips and shoulders in alignment is called *svikt*, which means weight, the bounce you make when skiing, the absorption of the body's weight into the earth as we dance, skate or ski. Svikt is the first principal of Nordic movement. When everyone is moving in svikt with the rhythm of the music and the earth, we achieve *tyngde* or wave. A skier in svikt moves in waves across the snow. A circle dance has tyngde when everyone is together in the energy of the dance. And from this combination comes *kraft* or power. This is the magical power of the earth coming up through the body that allows us to spin, leap, and gives a sense of flying. A halling tune says "var du ikke galen so flaut ikke so" or if you were not in a galder/frenzy you wouldn't fly like that. And it all starts with being in stav, in Isa.

Ice and fire were the two primordial elements of creation in Norse mythology. It is interesting today that the ice of glaciers and mountain ranges hold well-preserved treasures as varied as extinct plants and remains of our human ancestors. In fact, if you take a core sample of a glacier, you can read the öorlog of the entire earth. In this way I relate Isa to Urd, the keeper and preserver of the historical records of all existence, the primal law, öorlog.

Isa is tied to both creation and preservation. Before refrigerators, ice helped insure that food would stay fresh. Other associations with preservation come in the use of Isa as a bindrune. A bindrune is a combination of runes put together to create specific meaning and magic. We often see the rune Fehu (associated with wealth) combined with Isa to preserve resources. Many times it is paired with Gifu to help preserve the gift of a relationship.

Some people think ice means you are stuck and unmoving. Not at all true! Even glaciers are on the move. And look what changes they leave in their slow but steady wake. Ice also gives us the ability to move about in the winter where we could not move before…over water. If my friend lives on the other side of the lake and I have no boat, the only time I can visit her is in the winter by crossing the bridge of ice. Ice connects us to places that would be unreachable without it. So Isa also has associations with bridging and helps us to reaching new places in our lives. But beware! Anyone who has crossed a frozen lake knows how dangerous it can be.

The skills Isa calls to us are patience, discipline, caution, bravery, and good listening. Good listening? Yes. The ice may look perfectly safe, but there is a specific sound that can be heard just before it breaks, a strange dull thud followed by a sharp crack. There are a few seconds between the thud and the crack which can be the seconds that save one's life. I have heard this sound. Even breathing too hard can mask it. Fortunately, I was only crossing the shallow creek at my grandmother's farm the time I took the icy plunge. But one never forgets that sound. I think there must be a memory of it hidden in our ancient brains. It stirs such deep emotional response that it may be a genetic memory. It may be the sound of Ymir! The sound of a crack in the ice reverberates in our very marrow, the fear it can create may leave us paralyzed. But that inability to react could cost you your life!

Isa says listen to what others are saying and discern if it is the truth or not. There is a sound that Truth makes. It's solid and unwavering. It makes you feel relieved. The sound of falsehood is like a dull thud and a sharp crack, makes your stomach tighten up. Falsehood is thin and weightless, and if you do not heed the warning sounds you may fall prey to the deceptions and lies of others. I hear these thin, weightless sounds on television a lot. They disrupt my reptilian brain so I don't watch a lot of television. Good listening must be practiced. It requires quietness and stillness in body and brain. Shut off the chatter in your head that keeps you from really hearing the subtleties of words, actions, and all the sounds of the world.

When Isa comes up, I tell people to slow down, get into stav position. Walk in stav, quietly, in nature if possible. Listen to the sounds of the world, the birds, the melting snow, the rustle of leaves or grasses, the sound of rain. Everything has a sound, a tone, a voice in creation. This rune wants you to be still and quiet enough to hear the music around you and discern what is solid and what is dangerously thin. My good friend is what is called a "Death Walker." She helps people pass over to the other side, especially if they died in such a way that their body parts are not all in the same place. She describes the process of holding their tone for them so that they can collect all the DNA and genetic memory from all their parts. When they are ready, they unify with their tone and move off into the next world.

As a vocal teacher, I can relate to this. Everyone has a unique tone they make with their first breath. This is the birth tone that we strive to vibrate our bodies to as we sing, chant, and tone in meditation. Birth tone and death tone are the same. They are the unique sound of our own creation, our personal Ymir. Isa also has associations with Ansuz, the mouth of god and the mouth of the river, and with Laguz the lake, as well as with the frozen state of each of these. As the ice of our creation cracks we can hear our own tone. Listen for it often. Go quietly and slowly with patience and care. Then you can hear your unique tone, and the music of creation will be revealed to you.

12. Jera

Jera: phoneme j or y - year, the earth goddess Jord, harvest. The shape of Jera is Kenaz (to know) opening up to Kenaz reversed, with Kenaz eating the leg of Kenaz reversed. Its shape shows movement and is a cyclical, energetic symbol often found in decorative work around the globe. Ice melts, and springtime comes. The beginning of the harvest is in the planning.

Jera is a rune that anyone in farm country can relate to. Even city dwellers are reminded on the nightly news of the tenuous nature of creating a livelihood from farming, a pastime essential to us all. With droughts, floods, late frosts, hail, too little snow or fast melts, the quality of the harvest depends in large part on forces outside human control. For example, my ancestors farmed at a 45 degree slope on the side of Nedbergo, a mountain on the Sognefjord. Jera is a combination of skill, community support, force of will and divine help. It indicates a full year of preparation, nurturing, harvesting and preserving before you can really rest.

There is a saying, "You reap what you sow." Think of the seeds we plant, literally and metaphorically each day. Our words are seeds. As Ansuz, (the mouth rune) teaches us, a word can start a universe. In the Futhark, Jera comes after Isa, "the ice rune," which has already warned us to go slowly and be careful. In World time, the receding glaciers of the Ice Age left incredibly fertile land for the next phase of human activity. If we have gone slowly, made good decisions about what to plant, and been diligent about growing our crops, (and if the weather gods have favored us) we are prepared to reap the incredible reward of Jera, the harvest.

Though we harvest in the fall, Jera begins in February, right around groundhog's day. In heathen tradition, this is a time to "charm the plough." At this time we evaluate the seeds saved from the last harvest to see which ones have dried well and are still viable. Have some molded or shriveled into death with no life left to produce plants in the year to come? Did the mice get at them? Are they hardy heirloom seeds that can reproduce again and again or are they single-use-only hybrid seeds, useless to us the following spring? What has happened to our growing space over the last year? A downed tree can mean new full sun in our gardening beds. Excessive growth may mean we need to find more shade-tolerant varieties. In terms of our lives, how have we changed and grown over the last season or two? Do we need to drop old projects and begin new ones?

Jera asks us to take a look at the sum total of our own growing year, evaluate it with honesty and plan ahead for our future. By saying yes to only the things that we truly want to grow and discarding those things that no longer work for us, our whole year balances out. Jera is one of the runes that indicates a time line. *A year and a day* is the usual time given for an initiation process. A full harvest cycle begins with blessing the seeds and setting the intention. We prepare the soil, care for and nurture the crops, and ultimately - we hope - harvest. And the extra day? That is the day of the harvest celebration.

Harvest festivals are a common cultural tradition all over the world. Humans need to look at the hard work they have done, share the benefits throughout the community, and thank the gods it all worked out. In the Celtic agricultural calendar there are three harvest festivals. The first one in August celebrates the god of the grain who has given his life that we may have bread for the winter. The second one in September blesses the god of the fruit so the apples and grapes are pressed and bottled and celebrated. The third is the harvest of the meat in October. This is the beginning of winter when the herds are culled. If there are more animals than winter fodder, the weaker ones that will not make it through the winter are butchered. Autumn hunts happen at this time for bear, deer and elk. Meat is dried and stored. Hides are tanned and made ready to be worked into new boots. Bones and horns are cleaned and saved to make tools and instruments. The final shearing is done and the wool is carded for winter spinning and working. We feast, celebrate, and honor our four legged brothers and sisters for their selfless sacrifice.

In Norway, midwives are called jordmor - earth mothers. A birth is a year's harvest. In the old days the first trimester climaxed with the quickening, a mother's ability to feel the baby move. The second trimester was quickening to showing, and the third was showing to birthing. The three month period after the birth was the postpartum time sometimes called preserving. The health of the mother is preserved through rest and special foods. The health of the baby depended on this. The preservation of the baby physically was important as the ancients believed that "ensoulment" happens after the postpartum months have passed. Sometimes the baby would be swaddled with a piece of silver or runes or other charms to keep the baby from being stolen and replaced by huldre, hidden or underground folk. The baby was rarely given a name until after the full cycle was complete. It was acceptable to eliminate the baby during this three month period as well. If the resources of the family or community could not sustain another mouth to feed, babies could be exposed to the elements and left to die. This was, in the mind of the ancients, just.

People equate Jera with justice and legal orderliness. The adage "You reap what you sow" applies to the law of the land equally as well as the "laws of karma" or wyrd. The scales that weigh and measure our harvest of grain are the same ones used to measure our harvest of luck. It is the balance of Gebo in motion. In Norse tradition we can harvest luck through our diligent work and relationships. When the harvest is good we are said to have been blessed by or favored by the gods. This may relate to being favored by the judge in a court case. Yet ultimately, justice derives from the hard work people put into their lives. We must sometimes look at life retrospectively over the course of many seasons to fully understand the fairness of life. I often tell my children, when they say "that's not fair" that really, life *is* quite fair. We just need to live long enough to see it play out.

It may take more than one lifetime to balance the scales. Jera speaks also to the harvest of many lifetimes work. As Norse believed we were reborn into our own family öorlog, we have the opportunity to balance out any injustices our ancestors may have experienced or caused through paying *shild* (debt) such as going to Al-Anon meetings or working towards the restoration of polluted farmland or rivers. In the same way we must use the talents we inherited from them through practicing the crafts they handed down.

Jera is the goddess Jord (meaning Earth) and is the mother of Thor. Odin (meaning Spirit) the sky and Jord the earth combine to create the energy of lightening, Thor. It was believed that Thor's thunder would wake Jord from her wintery sleep. In the Baltic, Thor is called Perkuna and it was unlucky to begin preparing the earth for planting before the first thunderstorm. In the Thor stories we follow him through many situations that challenge his temper and his ability to be even-handed with is hammer. Eventually he won a seat at the well of Urd where the Aesir come to hold Thing, using his hammer to dispense justice according to Nornic law, a law based on that which aught, by necessity, to happen.

13. Eiwaz

Eiwaz: phoneme y - yew tree. As all three rune poems declare, yew trees are wonderful. Eiwaz is the evergreen in the runic alphabet. The only other tree represented in the Elder Futhark is Berkanan, the birch tree. The Younger Futhark added ash and oak as well. The yew is associated with immortality because of its longevity. There are 2,000-year-old yew trees still alive today! The yew is able to reproduce itself through branches that touch the ground and take root, becoming individual trees of their own. This technique of layering to reproduce is a metaphor for lineage, öorlog and partnerships. We help one another, giving of ourselves to create new complete individuals. Yews are sexed individually, one tree is male with cones that create pollen and one tree is female with flowers that are difficult to see until they ripen into bright red berries in the fall. So in some ways, this rune is another yin/yang or masculine/feminine combination.

Yew wood is hard, yet flexible. It was used in cabinet making, ship building (particularly masts) and can even be fashioned into nails. The most significant invention that came from yew wood was the longbow, a technology that, when it was new, was so profound that it changed the lives of people forever. Whether in war or hunting game, the longbow gave people the power to achieve goals that previously seemed impossible, but which, by means of focus and careful aim, came within their reach. Because the longbow makes us both strong and incredibly flexible, we can take bigger risks, knowing we will not break. We can see farther and shoot straighter and longer. This is important to remember when we are negotiating relationships and contracts and our own understanding of our capabilities. Eiwaz gives us strength and flexibility and reminds us to keep our roots in deep and branches high.

Linguistically Eiwaz has been related to the Yeoman (bowman). Unpacking from a trip recently, I received a visit from a fellow traveling artist and healer. I started going too fast, pulled a back muscle, and needed to ask for help. I was lucky to have had a powerful yeoman at my back, literally. This rune says you have one too. You just need to ask for assistance!

The yew is also a mystery tree, planted in graveyards and sacred places. It is sometimes planted for protection and takes a long time to mature. Its wood is also excellent for divining rods as it always seeks its mark, be it water, game or treasure. Many of the most ancient yews in Europe have roots that encompass small wells or springs, associating the yew with the world tree in Norse cosmology. The leaves of the yew grow in spirals, a visual representation of the cosmos, like the double helix of DNA and the other spirals of nature's design. The leaves are toxic, but decocted correctly they create a powerful drug for fighting cancer – Taxol.

In Celtic tradition, nine kinds of wood are gathered for the Beltane fires lit to cleanse and purge on the last night of spring (May eve). The yew would have been one of those trees pruned at the Solstice and burned at Beltane. Ancient people used yew in the fire to divine with numerology by the numbers of snaps and pops it gave. So, yew has numerological and magical energy.

Eiwaz is about planting firm roots for goal setting and focusing on the target. It's about trusting that you can hit your mark even if it seems out of reach. Trust that you will bend without breaking and that your yeoman will come when you ask for help. Healing, deep magic, and the ability to use these gifts are yours through Eiwaz.

66

14. Perth

Perth/Peord: the phoneme P - dice cup, luck, apple/pear, the vulva, the cave. There are so many possible meanings for Perth because there is no definitive word to connect to it linguistically. It looks like a dice cup tipped on its side, an opening, a vessel, a cave and the position of birthing. To me, this is the rune of the Norns, the volva, the spakona and the midwife.

The Anglo Saxon rune poem talks of Perth as a source of recreation where warriors sit together in the beer hall. This has in turn been interpreted as gaming or gambling. Gambling and gaming were commonplace in Nordic culture, perhaps because the northlands are a gamble of a place to live. Nature can turn on you in a moment, especially up on the fjords. My mother relates a story of the narrow pass between the farms on the fjord of her ancestors. It was a beautiful day, and a bridal party was passing through the gap when a sudden avalanche killed the whole lot of them. Gambling, casting lots, rolling the dice, is a way to exercise our luck. Gambling gives humans an energetic rush, a combination of fear, hope, anticipation, and even magical thinking. This is why gambling is second only to sex in the most difficult addictions to treat.

Two things to remember about the ancient Nordic mindset. First, the language lacks a future tense so the concept of destiny was quite different than the Greek definition as we understand it today. The only way to seek future insights is to immerse oneself in the knowledge of past precedence and ground oneself in the present moment. Then, drawing on the luck inherited through the öorlog, one may cast the runes, roll the dice, or read the signs of nature (such as birds flight) or sacrifice (such as entrails or blood splatters) to illuminate the likely possibilities or potentialities that determine immediate action (see divination section).

Second, luck is a living substance, part of our mind/body/soul complex. We inherit a certain amount of luck from our parents and their parents etc. through the öorlog. We can increase or decrease our luck through our deeds. Making wise alliances, keeping oaths, and living in an honorable way all increase our luck. Gambling becomes a way to "test" or "exercise" our luck, see if it is strong or weak. We need to remember that luck is neither good nor bad in and of itself. It is up to us to make our luck one way or the other through attitude, work ethic, and prayer.

In China they say luck is one fifth of a person's make up. Destiny, luck, feng shui, education, and philanthropy are the five pillars of life. We can create good luck for ourselves with education and knowledge of things at hand. Philanthropy creates luck because what we put out returns to us with increase and it honors the names of our ancestors to be generous. With feng shui, the arrangement of our environment maximizes good energy flow. Good feng shui fosters good luck. Perhaps, when you draw this rune it is time to evaluate your life, your home, and your relationships to see how your luck has been affected. It may be time to look into your heart and *öorlog* to see if you are following your highest purpose in life.

Our luck can be affected at the moment of our births with the visitation of the Norns, the wyrd sisters, the giant goddesses who tend the well of öorlog, *Urdarbrunnr,* and repair the roots of the world tree with layers of white clay from their well. The norns are compelled to come twice in our lives, at birth and at death. A theory put forth by Thorolf Wardle (Runelore) and expounded upon by Freya Aswynn (Northern Mysteries and Magick), two words were changed in the post-Christian reading of the Anglo Saxon poem. Read *wifan*, wives in place of *wigan*, warriors and *beorth*, birth in place of *beor*, beer. I am in agreement with these scholars as intuitively and through practical reasoning, Perth is a birth/death/re-birth rune of nornic power.

They are called *nornar naudigastir*, the norns who are the guests of need. It is still a custom in parts of Scandinavia to set out *nornargrøt* (norn porridge) to honor them when they visit the birthing room. They can increase luck and form the potential for a happy and prosperous life. Of course, the opposite is also true. In the classic tale of Sleeping Beauty, one Norn was not invited to the christening. It was disastrous for the child princess, her parents, and the country she represented.

In the Voluspa (first poem of the poetic Edda) the seer remembers when the three giant women, wise in all things, came into being. Urd is the first of these three sisters. Her name means that which is. With the root word *ur*, she is primal and ancient, she sits at the well named for her. She knows the history of all things and seers must work intimately with her to comprehend the fullness of the past. The past is all we can truly know and it creates the present moment of becoming. Each strand of individual öorlog is held on her spindle and these individual lines connect in a pattern of existence called the Web of Wyrd.

Verðandi (Verthandi or Verdandi), the second sister, means becoming, the present moment, the now. This is where we live (or strive to live), in the now. Before any divination or action that counts on luck, we must ground ourselves in the past and center ourselves in the present. There is a special feeling, as though all things are locked into place and consciousness expands to include everything when one is in the full awareness of the present moment. You will see gamblers and gamers perform various rituals from blowing on the dice to kissing a fetish in order to achieve "one-ness" with their luck in the moment of Verthandi. Seers must achieve a deep connection with Verthandi that unifies them with the world tree and the nine worlds held therein. Yngona Desmond in her book, "Vøluspa: Seidr as Wyrd Consciousness" calls this a seidr state, a deep connection with past and now that allows a seer to glimpse more of the wyrd web than her own small strand. Her *spå* (prophecy) is only as good as her knowledge of past and ability to be present and see the potential within the wyrd.

In the old days when everyone had to join in the spinning of wool or flax into thread and yarn, the meaning of the Norns was illustrated in this daily task. Urd is that which has been spun, Verthandi is the point where the spun and un-spun rove meet. We hold onto this point until the un-spun rove is drafted out to the desired thickness, then let go. The un-spun rove becomes the past. The future is never created, only the past is created in layer upon layer ad infinitum.

So what of Skuld, the third sister? Her name translates to necessity and shild (debt), what we owe to the past, our ancestors and divinities, for our very existence. Skuld sheds the light on and directs us in the creation of past and present through necessity. It is our responsibility to draft out the rove to the best possible thickness based on what by necessity ought to become. She can guide us into proper action but it is up to us to do the work. Skuld is also listed first in the line of Valkyries, the goddesses who come at the moment of death. Birth and death and the invariable re-birth into our family lineage are guided by the norns and are represented in the rune Perth. The fallen fruit is the end of the process for the apple or pear, and the seeds of the next tree are within. The vulva, the womb, the cave and the cauldron are all symbols of the birth, death and re-birth process that the norns regulate along with Hel whose road we must all walk (unless we die in battle and are collected by Freya or Odin).

In the Voluspa, the norns are said to be *skáru á skíði*, scoring or etching marks, possibly runes, on wood. As humans were created from trees, this verse is often taken to mean that they score the runes in our bones. We each hold within our bones and blood the runes (perhaps in the form of DNA) that will determine our "future." For example, if we will have brown or blue eyes, if we will be able to digest alcohol or milk, if we will be prone to heart attack and all the other inheritances we receive (see Othila). It goes on to say, *þær lög lögðu, þær líf kuru alda börnum, örlög seggja*, they write down the laws, they choose lives, of all who are born their öorlog speak. The norns keep the "Akashic" records. Perth can be used to access these records, to access your own personal historical öorlog, and to view the totality of your wyrd.

70

This is what the newly added "blank rune" attempts to convey quite redundantly. Perth speaks to the Norns already. Check the surrounding runes for help in deciding how you should draft out your next bit of rove. Ask yourself these questions: Am I repeating old patterns that do not serve my highest good? Are there broken or tangled threads in my life that I need to repair and smooth? Have I added to my store of luck or is my luck running out?

When Perth comes up, it can indicate that one should take "the road less traveled." Try a non-traditional approach to your issue! Take a gamble on a new direction. If what you "have always done" has not worked, do the opposite. Make your decision by flipping a coin. In this way Perth is another journey rune. It presents us with the option to trust our luck and travel a new path. Often Perth indicates that it is time for the questioner to explore the great unknown of occult knowledge or "the left hand path." This phrase relates to the right brain way of knowing. The female, intuitive pathway is stressed in this rune, as with Laguz, but in a different way. Laguz (the lake) is about getting to know your shadow self, your womb self, your female or goddess within. Perth is less about getting to know it as it is about throwing it up to see where it lands. Where Laguz says explore the coin, Perth says flip it!

It is the rune of the crone. In decades of giving rune readings to the public this rune rarely comes up. Not many people seem drawn to pick this one. When it does, it is almost always drawn by older women who are ready to take on the mantle of wise woman. Remember, this rune is housed in the aett of Hel. It is powerful, ancient, and deep.

Perth doesn't mean throw caution to the wind, but too much caution and too much thought/logic, may have blocked your ability to see alternatives. Perth wants us to look outside the box of our normal options and take a risk on an alternative approach. It comes up in questions of medical proceedings, suggesting remedies that are out of the Western medical model. It wants us to ground in the knowing of the past, center in the present moment, and bravely draft out our öorlog with our deepest determination to follow the flow of necessity where ever it leads us.

15. Algiz

Algiz, Ehol: phoneme z - elk, sedge Like Perth, Algiz is a controversial rune for meaning. It has most commonly been related to a word meaning Elk or Elk-god. It has associations with protection and defense. Some authors have even called it the eagle rune. I generally call it protection and relate elk, caribou, and deer to it. The antler god in Norse tradition would be Freyr who lives on the border between domestic and wild, infusing farm life with the energy of the hunt. He gave up his Iron sword for the love of a giant woman. This left him only a stang (antler strapped to a spear) for a weapon at Ragnarok. The shape of Algiz looks like a deer's antler. It is a Y with the center pole extending beyond the V, a shape seen throughout nature in trees and other plants.

It has also been called Eolh-sedge, a very sharp edged grass growing in marshes and fens, relating this rune to Frigg whose hall is Fensalir, hall in the marsh. This rune is related to Laguz as, from the Anglo-Saxon rune poem, sedge "grows in the water and makes a ghastly wound" to warriors who touch it. There is a warning within this verse that the marshes and lakes, places of the goddess and feminine divine, should not be carelessly entered. Masculine energy, force, must be submissive to care and gentle nature to gain the wisdom within the feminine/water.

I call this the prayerful rune as I make this shape each time I wake and stretch my palms heavenward. I also call this the rune of willingness each time I throw my hands into the air and exclaim, "I don't know. I give up!" Sometimes I need to give up on something in order to remove my ego and willfulness from the situation. Then I relax and become willing to look at the problem a different way. This *willingness over willfulness* is the essence of this rune in many ways. A wise woman once told me that when I pray for things I should say, "this or something better." That phrase gets my limited and pre-conceived notions about what ought to happen and how it ought to happen out of the way so that my *disr* and guides can work for me in ways I never would have imagined. Algiz asks us to stop micro-managing relationships and processes in our lives. This is the message of elk.

Jamie Sams tells a story about the elk in her book Animal Medicine Cards. The elk was the first of our animal kin to recognize that the humans were hairless and would die in the cold of the coming ice age. The elk sacrificed itself that we might wear its skin and eat its meat and use its every part. Elk was willing to do this for us, and we respected it deeply. We followed the elk herd. We collected grasses and other plants so to feed the herd so they wouldn't have to work as hard. This was an early symbiosis, a relationship that was not quite domestication and not all together wild. In this story both the elk and the sedge grass are represented in the bargain.

As eagle, Algiz is the messenger of the gods in Native American stories, asking humans to give up on their ego-influenced ways of hearing and perceiving and to listen to the voice of Great Spirit. In Norse tradition, a giant in eagle form sits atop the world tree. His wings blow the cosmic winds. Eagle connects the sky and earth in a profound way. We must connect in this way too. We must ground ourselves to the Earth but still reach for the stars with arms uplifted, be the tree - and we must have faith and trust that we will hear the messages of the tree, the eagle, or the four wind deer nipping at the branches.

In the Younger Futhark, the shape of this rune is inverted and replaces Eiwaz, the yew. It is called Yr, the yew with three roots digging deep into the three lower worlds and the wells below. As with all the runes, the position of Algiz in the Futhark alphabet informs its meaning. It follows the uncertainty of Perth, the luck rune. When we take the risk or leap of faith Perth suggests, Algiz is the process of letting go of control, feeling protected and becoming willing. The result is the next rune, Sowilo, the strength of the sun itself!

16. Sowilo

Sowilo, Sol, Sigel, Sunna, Saule: phoneme s - literally means the goddess Sun. Coming after Algiz, Sowilo ends the middle string of the Futhark. The middle aett begins with Hagal (hail) and continues to need, ice, earth, yew, luck, elk and then, at long last, the triumph of the sun. It's important to remember this order because of the hardship and change that comes before Sowilo. The shape of Sowilo is like a lightning bolt or a ray of the sun shining down. When I see it a little tune of triumph comes into my head - like "ta da!"

In the Northlands, weeks, even months may go by without sunshine or blue sky. It is often dark, grey, and cold. Yet everyone knows Sun is essential to life, mental and physical health. Sun is a powerful rune for energy, strength, health and life. In the Icelandic rune poem she is called the "destroyer of ice", a welcome relief from many long months of Winter. This rune can be used to break through a stagnant or fallow period in life or in a project.

In Scandinavian/Germanic myth, the Sun was the goddess Sol/Sunna, daughter of Mundilfari (Turner of Time). Sunna drives the sun disk across the sky in her chariot drawn by the two horses All Swift and Early Waker. Her brother is Mani, who draws the moon across the sky more slowly. Both are chased by chaos wolves who will gobble them up if they do not stay on their courses. This rune is for the strength to endure and keep the course.

Sunna was the original working mother. She had but two days off each year, at Winter and Summer solstices. Her husband was Glenr (opening in the clouds) who would bring their daughter to visit in the chariot while Mani stayed unmarried and was considered the father to all Midgard's children.

Sowilo is a hard-working rune. It energizes one to complete tasks, to press on. It gives hope in the darkest winter hours and abundant blessings on the longest day of the year. Sunna and Mani both played important roles in the lives of hard-working farmers. Their roots as deities go back at least 4 thousand years to the Bronze Age, where symbols for Sun and Moon adorn rock petroglyphs, grave goods, and are found in the bogs where many Bronze Age religious items appear to have been deliberately submerged. Nerthus was the bog goddess and these items could have been sacrifices to her. After all, the Earth Mother needs the Sun in order to generate life.

The Baltic tribes mingled with Scandinavian and Germanic tribes during the Bronze Age. The Baltic sun goddess is Saule and her hymns and chants and spiral dances are still sung today in Latvia and Lithuania. My favorite Lithuanian chant is "Saulala motula, užtekėk, užtekėk" which roughly translates to "Sun goddess, mother, wheel across the sky so we can have enough." Spirals and swastikas (the original symbols for the sun in most ancient cultures) are formed by dancers holding torches, lighting up the dark solstice sky with her symbols and songs.

Sunna's most precious times are the solstices, solstead in Anglo-Saxon meaning the day the Sun goes home. At solstice wheels are taken off of vehicles and dressed up, everyone stays in the stead. Sometimes they are lit on fire and rolled down hills and fjords. All spinning must stop and all mills stand still. This is the only rest Sunna gets, and no one is to disturb her from resting on these days. This might be a message for the "work-a-holic" who would push their work hours into what should be hours of resting and holiday making. Remember the old saying about all work and no play making you dull, depressed, and grumpy (or worse).

Fire goddesses are enjoying resurgence in popularity these days, especially for their importance as sun goddesses. I think this is significant in human development because, since the advent of patriarchal societies, women have been associated with the "weaker" light of the moon and men with the strong light of the sun. We balance our psychology when we realize the strength of women's fire power. Equally important is understanding the moon gods, encouraging men's psychic and mysterious cycles to be nurtured as well.

As you can well see, Norse tradition is full of male and female balancing. Dag, the god of Day, heralds Sunna's coming, Nott the goddess of Night heralds Mani. This rune could be asking you to find the balance of your own masculine and feminine powers.

A lot of people want to know "how long it will be" until their situation changes or until they get what they are seeking. While the runes don't work on a linear time line, this rune may advise us to watch for answers by the next Solar Holiday (equinox or solstice). Sometimes answers come more immediately at these threshold times of year. I also suggest that people may want to wake at the first light and greet Sunna as she rides over the horizon. The clarity of the moment in this threshold time is magical. This is a time of strength to be used and enjoyed, not wasted.

When I draw Sowilo I am uplifted. Simply putting a jaundiced child in a sunny window can heal the sickness. It's how we get our Vitamin D. Sowilo asks us to be observant of our health and strength and encourages us to use its power to gain more of the same. It may also indicate a peak time of creative energy. Think of the fire of life hiding within a single seed. All it needs to become a full plant is contained within. And the strength of the sun can hasten the most stubborn seeds to sprout. This is the power of Sowilo, the impetus to flourish. Respect this power and do not let it pass unused!

Tyr/Zisa's Aett

"Isaz on the Baltic" photo by David de Young, Helsinki, Finland 2014

Making rune shapes with the body is natural and intuitive. The ice rune is a single stav, easy to make with the body, it calms and centers us. It puts anxiety "on ice" and produces a sense of balance and well-being. In the Elder Futhark, some runes require a stick or another body to create. In the Younger Futhark all rune shapes are stav and can be created by one person.

17. Tiwaz

Tiwaz/Tyr: phoneme t - literally means god. In Norse myth it is specifically the one handed god Tyr, also the spear and the distaff. Tyr looks like an arrow or a spear. It's made from Isa, the straight line, with a point like Kenaz topping it off. It is Laguz and Laguz's reflection. Tyr is the first rune of the final aett, the last leg of our journey through the Futhark.

The Anglo Saxon rune poem calls Tyr the guiding star which never fails on its course. Its shape resembles the compass needle, an arrow pointing to the North Star guiding the seafaring folk of the Northlands. Tyr means focus, direction, determination, guidance and a steady course. Tyr is a protection rune. Knowing where you are and where your ship is headed can help keep you out of danger. Remaining calm and focussed is essential to your protection. Tyr is called glory or victory and was a popular rune for funeral urns and sword hilts.

In one story Tyr is the son of a giant named Hymir, which makes him an old god and of Jotun blood. His name is ancient and derives from the Sanskrit *deva* (god) and the Indo-European chief god Dyeus. Tacitus describes him as chief of the gods, though Odin and Thor surpassed him in popularity by the later Iron Age and Snorri calls him the son of Odin.

Some of the ancient Germanic tribes described a female consort or twin deity of Tyr (who was Ziu in Old High German) named Zisa. As he points to the heavens, she points to the earth. Tacitus equates her with Isis, and she shares many of the same attributes of other god/goddess pairings. She is the all-mother, devoted wife, patroness of nature and magic. She carried the staff, and her name meant throne or high seat. She is a goddess of the birth, death, and re-birth cycle. Her priests and priestesses were prophets and healers and had the power to control nature's elements through braiding and unbraiding their hair and through knot magic.

Many of these attributes are held by Freya (twin of Freyr) and Frigg (wife of Odin). The shape of this rune is like is a distaff, a long stick at least three feet in length (also called a stave) with a finial or fork on the end, used to hold the un-spun fibers of flax or wool for spinning. Here again are associations with focus, control, and direction, literally as in the spinning process, but metaphorically as well. Spinning is a trance-inducing activity which often led women into vocalizing predictions for the future. The Eddas and Sagas (ancient Norse and Icelandic stories) described the völva (staff carrying women) carrying distaffs as they traveled from village to village doing trance work, healing, and foretelling of the futures potential. The völva held the fibers of the universe steady as they spun out the details of the fates of the village and its people. Some distaffs mentioned in the stories carried magical powers. People "tapped" with a distaff might fall into deathly sickness, though the Sagas suggest such curses were done in self-defense. The use of long and often heavily weighted poles in martial arts would also have played a role in the lives of these nomadic women.

Martial arts use also brings us back to Tyr as a symbol of protection in battle. In the Icelandic rune poems Tyr is called the "leavings of the wolf" both as a reference to battle glory and in reference to the story of how Tyr lost his sword hand. In the stories, Tyr was a companion to Fenrir the chaos wolf, one of Loki's children. While playing with chaos and chaotic people can be fun and energizing, when it gets in the way of safety and security for the community, it's time to stop playing. Fenrir played an essential role in Ragnarok, the fall of the gods and the destruction of the Earth and all the worlds at the end of time. The gods wanted to bind Fenrir and keep him from causing this destruction. The only way to hold the wolf steady was for someone to put their hand in his mouth. If the gods betrayed the wolf, that god would lose his hand. Tyr knew that he was the one who must sacrifice part of himself. Losing his sword hand he then had only a spear at the battle of Ragnarok. It is the rune of keeping our word, no matter what the cost.

Tyr holds the meaning of justice and judicious sacrifice to serve the greater good. It is also important that he did not lose his life. The lesson is that is important to sacrifice for the greater good, but one need not sacrifice everything. Find out exactly what is required and how much you are capable of. Be honest with yourself and feed the cause only as much as necessary to keep your thread steady while feeding the whole. Keep chaos at bay through your focus, diligence, and determination!

Finally, there is a sense of balance and honesty in this rune. Tyr asks us to focus on our place in the Universe and be guided by it as the North Star guides a ship. Tyr reminds us that the yang side of our being, the thrusting arrow, is also the yin side of the distaff that holds the stuff of our making in place as our lives spin out. Tyr says: stay the course, steady as she goes, give only as much as needed, trust your intuition and protect yourself and others with these virtues.

18. Berkanan

Berkanan, Berkana, Bjarken: phoneme b - birch tree, birth, life and death cycle. Berkanan is the second of two tree names in the rune alphabet. (Eiwaz, the yew, is the first and Perth as apple tree may also be considered here.) Berkanan looks like a B but with pointy Kenaz spikes rather than rounded ones up against the straight line of Isa. It comes in the final aett after the twins Tyr and Zisa. The Germanic goddesses Pertcha or Berchta (the sound of their names is similar to birch and birth) have been linked to Birch. These goddesses are linked to Freya and Frigg of the Scandinavians through their activities related to birth/death/rebirth cycles, healing, herding, spinning and communication with the other worlds.

In Norway the birch lur was a herding woman's horn. This conical overtone horn was used in the Fjordlands by the women who tended the sæter (upland summer farms) to communicate with the animals and one another, blow songs of praise or warn of danger. There are stories of young women whose sæters were overcome by bandits and under the pretext of calling in the herds, the women summoned help from the valley through the lur.

The Birch was and still is a sacred, goddess, life-line tree in all Northern circumpolar cultures. In their book, "Celebrating Birch: The Lore, Art, and Craft of an Ancient Tree" (2007), the North House Folk School up in Northern Minnesota, teaches about all aspects of the birch. Ecologically, birch is the tree of regeneration. When the old forest is cleared of hardwoods by lumbering, fire or ice flows, the birch is the first to return. Because of its ability to give birth to a new habitat, the birch is called the Mother tree or Nursery tree. It protects the new hard woods until they can take over. When the hard wood takes over and the nursemaid is no longer needed, they die in place and are called the "standing dead," still useful and preserved in their birch bark tombs. When they do fall, they become the undergrowth that the hard woods depend upon to gain their might, hight and strength.

Birch bark has multiple ritual uses. I often write prayers on the bark paper and send them through the flames. Birch is sacred to the sauna (Finno-Ugric) or pirtz (Baltic) steam bath rituals. Bundles of birch leaves are used to slap the skin to stimulate circulation and waken up the senses. There is a runo in Votic (Finno-Ugric), a ritual whisking of the bride and sauna song. There they use three birch twigs and five thin switches before sprinkling the hot rocks with sacred waters.

Birch oil is used to stimulate circulation, prevent and treat frost bite. It is anti-microbial, anti-viral and antiseptic. It is used topically for skin disorders. Birch sap is collected for a spring tonic full of minerals and can be boiled down like Maple sap to use as a sweetener in the kitchen. Leaves and twigs can be boiled for tea. The oldest birch near swamps grow a fungus called chaga that is harvested, ground and used for teas and tinctures for many health complaints including cancer.

Birch provides firewood and kindling (burns even when wet), wood for bowls, buckets, toys and tools. The bark is woven into mats, baskets, and even shoes, used in water craft and building materials. Birch bark is still used in Norway for roofs with plots of turf to hold it down and a goat or two up on top to keep the grass trimmed. Idyllic! A tæga is a special basket made from its roots in Norwegian tradition.

Berkanan is dear to my heart as a native Minnesotan. Just the sight of a birch grove in any season is breathtakingly beautiful. In winter they are white and black next to blood red dogwood, yellow and red willow and the occasional crimson flash of a cardinal. The dark blue/green of pine in the distance increases the contrast. In summer, standing in a birch grove transports one to the world of Faerie. Sun streams through the light foliage in rays of glory. Beneath the birches, mossy soft ground tempts us to lie down and watch the dance of light. The slightest breeze sets the leaves to whispering all the secrets of the universe. In the fall the leaves are golden, and like the Brisingamen (Freya's necklace) they fall, spiraling to the upturned admirer. Birch was my great grandmother's favorite tree. The smell of a birch calls up memories from the most ancient parts of my brain.

When I journey (gandreid), I often begin in the birch grove as it is a border tree between worlds. From the line of birch I can follow the downward slope to Frigg's hall, Fensalir (marsh hall). I can go deeper into the grove as it opens up to Folkvanger (field of the folk), where Freya has her hall, Sessrumnir (many seats). I can go back through the grove and enter the pines to find the path to Helheim and the cave mouth to the underworld. I may follow the birch up the mountain. They get smaller and more twisted the higher I climb until I find the door to the dvereger (dwarves). Dveregeskog means dwarf birch thicket in Norwegian.

Berkanan is abundance, usefulness, beauty, birth, regeneration, and healing. Berkanan is communication through writing, music, ritual and trance work, and blessings to humans from the goddess. It asks us, what part of the journey are we in? New growth, nurse maid or standing dead?

19. Ehwaz

Ehwaz: phoneme e (eh) – horse. This rune is made with Isa, Kenaz opening to the sky and then Isa again. It comes after Berkanan (the birch tree) and before Mannaz (human kind).

The horse changed the face of every land and all people it came to. In the same way, Ehwaz changes things utterly. Horses gave us the ability to travel great distances, and using them in agriculture changed how much we could plow, haul and transport. The Vikings were said to trade walrus ivory for the horses that came out of Latvia (the land of my father's people). The Latvians have a god for horses and honey bees, called Usins. Horses, like honey bees, develop a psychic connection with their human companions. Horses are the only prey animal to develop this deep connection to a predator (humans).

Horses also changed the face of war because they could transport warriors farther faster. Warriors fighting on horseback were elevated above the fray of battle, and generals commanding from this height had a distinct advantage. The use of horses changed the communities of Mannheim (human home) forever.

Horses were sacred to every culture they came to. Many of the Norse gods had horses special to them, the most famous was Odin's eight legged Sleipnir who could ride between the worlds and even jump the fire wall of Hel's gate. Two horses hauled the chariot carrying the sun disk across the sky with Sunna at the reins. Each celestial being had a horse - Night, Day, and the Moon. Horses are magical, seeming to float over the earth when they run. There was a herd of horses that belonged to no one but the gods could sometimes ride them to Urd's well for councils there.

Ehwaz speaks to us of the changes that occur when a new and powerful element is introduced into our lives. Berkanan, the birch tree, presages the coming of that something new. In many ways, towards the end of our years, we undergo a re-birth of our selves. The crone, for example, comes close to becoming the maiden again. I look forward to the time in my life when the responsibilities of motherhood are eased and the children leave my side to build their own families. Then I can trade my van (Raido) for a motorcycle (Ehwaz)!

When Ehwaz appears, total change is on the horizon. It is situated in the last aett, the aett that describes us in our late life. Sometimes when people retire, they make drastic changes. They may move to Arizona or Florida, for example, or some other warm climate. They may start doing artwork or taking classes for fun. They may take up other hobbies they were not able to do while burdened with middle life responsibilities like raising families and living out their early life decisions. Ehwaz aids us in achieving a new level of freedom. Horses have often been associated with the life of the cowboy, freedom, the open range, and possibility. Sometimes, our later years are when the wisdom of the crone or wise man begins to manifest.

The Nordic people raise their own breed of horses. Icelandic "ponies" and fjord horses have strong shorter legs so they can more easily calculate the steep terrain. The ancient Norse looked to the horse for answers to mysterious questions or to decide on the solutions to controversial issues. In an Icelandic movie I once saw, a woman used a horse race to decide whether or not to marry a man from another clan. And I have read about a pure white horse that was kept in the village for the sole purpose of divination. Counting snorts and stomps, the priest would be able to make decisions for the community. The skull of a horse was sometimes attached to the bow of a longship as a way to curse the on-coming traffic. In the Vedas, we hear of the horse head that whispers secrets - hence the saying that "I got it straight from the horse's mouth." Even horse shoes were said to hold luck or ward off wicked sorcerers. However you look at it, Ehwaz is a harbinger of profound change. It forecasts travel, freedom, a greater ability to do new things and has associations with divination and inner wisdom. It is about taking up our power and going for it!

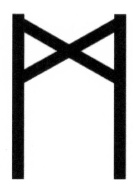

Mannaz, Madr: phoneme m - man or mankind, human home is Mannheim, community. Mannaz is one of my favorite runes. A true community will always include children and the elderly, those who either don't have enough to give yet or have already given their all. They are the small stavs crossing Naudiz, the need rune. But when we put them together in the center of community, they make the little Gebo, balancing one another and being held aloft by those strong stavs on either side. The ice runes of caution, care and preservation hold the relationship of our past (elders) and our future (children) up high. Mannheim is the gift of human relationships in Midgard, the world made for humans by the gods.

In most creation stories, the Divine creates humans and our world. But it is left to us to create Mannheim (community). In her book, "Cattle: An informal social history," Laurie Winn Carlson points out that the way prey animals gather in protection helped humanity to discover social order. In the Ice Age cave paintings at Mira, the calves and nursing cows are in the center, the mating pairs are in the next ring, and the strong bulls face the four quarters in protection. It is through community that we are able to survive, grow and discover our highest potential. Through community we evolve. And in community we have the opportunity to express our own divine nature through generosity, cooperation, philanthropy, and participation.

Thinking about our ancestors illustrates how important relationships are to survival. Individuals cannot grow all the food and create all the housing, tools, and clothing they need. Division of labor, barter and trade, education and spirituality, diverse and intergenerational parts taking care of each other are essential elements that create a thriving humanity. There is no more important concept than Mannheim, especially in these modern times.

I've heard many people express concern that we are losing our Mannheim because we no longer create what we need to survive through community relationships. Meeting our basic needs outside the community can lead to isolationism. Instead of taking care of and learning from our children and elderly we are institutionalizing them. This creates a multitude of disorders in our culture, of which depression and anxiety are the most benign. Even the Internet, despite its ability to link people together around the globe, can further contribute to the fragmentation of community if people no longer look to each other for information. This cuts them off from getting all sides of a story. If people can simply "Google it" and get what they need (or agree with) without personal contact, the intimacy of Mannheim can be lost. Elders may not feel useful and children may receive information without understanding the intimate traditions that connect and make it meaningful.

In writing this book, I have observed Mannheim working in my life. I am only writing it because I have a friend who wants to read it. Though I have learned much in the process, it is not for me. This book is for everyone. I am thankful every day that I am part of a community and family that supports me in doing my best work. And that's the heart of this rune. When you draw Mannheim, look around to see who is supporting you and in what ways they are doing so. Find the community network that feeds your highest good, and see what you can contribute to it. This is the cycle of a healthy social system.

Mannaz comes in the middle of the third aett. After Ehwaz (the horse rune) has taken us to our later years, we find Mannaz. Sometimes it is only when something drastic or strange has happened that we really

90

see and appreciate the support of our community. As Ehwaz predicted, we now have a new vision of who we are and what we are supposed to do with the wisdom. Bring it back to the community, become the wise elder, help others make their transitions! After that, Laguz will help us recede into the lake of self-discovery on a deeper level.

As an educator, I participated in workshops at the Science Museum of Minnesota regarding teaching the Native American population in our state. A professor from the Department of American Indian Studies at the University of Minnesota explained to us that these children, from the standpoint of their own culture, do not understand the concept of cheating. They do not consider intellectual property issues or competition when it comes to finding the answers to questions. When the Great Spirit gives an answer to one child, he or she shares it so that all have access to the knowledge.

This is what it means to live in a true community instead of in a hierarchy. In a community we gladly share our resources. Your joys are my joys, your sorrows are my sorrows, and your children are my children. No one is left alone or unsupported. No one dies in obscurity unmourned. In Norse tradition, community is the *innangard*, the inner farm. Everything in the innangard is considered whole, healthy, hail. Everything utgard (outside the community) is dangerous, suspect, un-whole until it is tested by the innangard.

Supporting all members of the community is also at the the root of the Abrahamic traditions, Judaism, Islam, and Christianity. Tithing (the gifting of ten percent of one's income) is just one example in those traditions of the command to support all members of the community. In Chinese philosophy, philanthropy is one of the five pillars the whole human along with destiny, luck, education, and feng shui. It is in the love of humanity that we reach our full potential as humans. This rune is asking you to identify your community, figure out if it is supporting you and if not, find one that does. Mannaz wants to know if you are giving and receiving in balance with your community. Are you engaged, volunteering and in a reciprocal relationship with neighbors, leaders, and family members? Get Gebo with self, get Mannaz with everyone else!

21. Laguz

Laguz: phoneme l water, lake, possibly lakuz or leek - all three rune poems talk about the various forms of water essential to life, travel and beauty in the Northlands. Laguz looks like a fishing spear, an arrow with only one tip side, a fishing hook or a broken reed. The ocean is the highway for boats but what is underneath can terrify. in terms of the leek, once again, it is the hidden portion of this onion cousin that is tender and flavorful. Laguz is asking us to look beneath the surface of things.

Between Mannaz (humankind) and Ing (the fertility twins) Laguz is one of my favorite runes. And coming from Minnesota, the land of 10,000 lakes, I really relate to it! When you grow up by a body of water you get to know it well. The shallows, drop offs, currents, beaches and shoreline all become special. Certain fish and other creepy crawlers, sea weeds, rocks and shells are particular to that lake. Sommer's Lake at my grandmother's farm was famous for its shallows and sudden drop off as well as an abundance of leeches. Parts of the shoreline harbored water snakes, and wild rice grew on the Northeast side.

The lake is a metaphor for the womb, and there is a Lady of the Lake in nearly every European mythology. There were beings associated with every form of water. In Scandinavia, fossegrimin are the spirits of waterfalls, nykken are the shore-line and sea trolls, and sjörå, ladies who were wardens of the lakes. Maintaining a relationship to these beings meant they would not lure you into their watery homes. It might even mean they would teach you to play nature's magical music, giving musicians the power over dancers and the hearts of listeners. But this means balance in relationships because dealings with these creatures can cause mental instability. Water conducts energy and changes emotions - water is emotion and this is a lesson of Laguz.

The lake is birth/death/re-birth and the womb. In Norse myth and practice, the wagon of Nerthus was driven into the lake and washed ceremonially after her festival. Archeological evidence suggests that those washing the wagon were ritually drowned in the lake. Sacrifices were often made to bodies of water like rivers, lakes and bogs. One type of Viking burial involved loading up a ship with necessary things (and people), lighting it on fire and sending it out on the lake, fjord or ocean. Lakes are associated with death because the lake is also the womb from which life springs. The ancients understood that death and birth are two sides of the same coin and completely dependent on one another. One cannot die without being reborn, and one cannot be born without the certainty of death.

The wisdom of Ansuz, the mouth of the river, the mouth of god, flows into Laguz, the lake, contributing to the collection of wisdom that has multiple levels. The deeps of the lake may be inhabited by strange sea monsters or giant fish with large teeth. The shallows may hold a quick current with an undertow that can easily sweep you away. Laguz asks you to explore your womb knowledge, to discover the depths of your right brain, your feminine, intuitive and yin side. In fact, scientists have found brain tissue on the spine in the areas of the heart and the gut. So when we say, "I know it in my gut" or "My heart tells me so," it's quite true.

Whether male or female we must all accept that we have intuition and a knowing that goes beyond simple reasoning into a realm of feeling and faith. We must come to terms with this if we are ever to be whole as humans. Whole, integrated self is what the next rune, Ing/Ingvine promises. But we must do the work to get there. Laguz suggests that you are ready to trust your gut.

The lake is pictured in the west of the Medicine Wheel in some Native American traditions. It is the place of sunset and dream time, the land of the witches. Perhaps Laguz is asking you to look at your dreams. If my attention to my dream diary wanes I find my dreams become more pressing and strange. As I become more diligent in writing down my dream observations I notice they become more mundane and easier to fit into my awake time. Just as modern humans put less emphasis on dreams – many say they are meaningless ramblings altogether - so too they denigrate feelings, intuition, and extrasensory perception.

Nordic culture held dreams as actual realities in which we are intimately involved. These realities continue on when we are awake, and part of us remains in the dream time (just as Karl Jung proposes). Since we spend one third of our lives sleeping and dreaming, it makes sense to pay attention and not waste the information we can cull from our dreams. There is an ancient tradition in every culture regarding the study, use and purpose of dreams.

Laguz is our psychic sense, but it can be tricky. You may think the surface is glassy and calm but what of the undertow? The key is to not let your fears of the unknown defeat you in your search of yourself as the lake. Don't take anything at face value. Look deeply and carefully at what you see, hear, and understand. Go cautiously into the lake, but do not allow your senses to be clouded with fear. Do not presume you can just barge your way into the female mysteries of Laguz or you may find yourself injured by the cut grass reeds protecting the borders. Laguz hints of a dangerous but necessary course of discovery.

In Minnesota, the lake was the lifeline. It's where we fished, gathered cat tails, wild rice, and other wild foods. It was where we washed our bodies and utensils. In modern times the lake is still where we sit and dream, and see the reflections of the moon and stars and the wide washes of color from sunsets and sunrises. Lakes provide irrigation and stability for agriculture and therefore, civilization. Mannaz, human kind or community comes before Laguz, suggesting that community is seeking the best place to thrive. My ancestors living on Sognefjord counted on the deep cold waters for so much of their livelihood, and their descendents, my relatives still living there, count on the fjord for tourism and trade.

Laguz asks us to explore and develop our woman/womb sense and pay attention to the messages on both the surface and the depths. It suggests we look more deeply into the matter we are questioning, just as the fisherman or woman would look for the best places to fish on the lake. Laguz gives us a hook or spear to throw and the strength to pull it up again if we are not afraid. It reminds us that we are the lake, and that the monsters dwelling within are also us. Both the rewards of living lakeside and the inherent dangers present in a large body of water are ours if we integrate this rune within ourselves. Death and life, and death and rebirth are our fate. Take care, but still enjoy.

22. Ingwaz

Ingwaz, Ing, Yngvi: phoneme ng - Lord an earlier name of Freyr, Yngvi-Frey, Lord of the Vanir. The Ingaevones and the Ynglinga tribes take their names from this rune, this deity. Danish and Swedish royal lines trace their lineage to the god and an ancient chieftain named for him. So, everything about Fehu and Freyr are included in this rune, including Freya - the lady. (It is also a rune in my last name which I could simply spell with the two runes - Tyr and Ing).

This is one of the oldest symbols used in textiles, pottery and bone carvings as old as the Neolithic. Sometimes the shape is represented by only the lozenge or diamond in the middle, a very ancient symbol for the mother goddess, the Yoni, Ganungagap, the gaping void of creation out of which everything flows. It is given the meaning fertility of Lord and Lady. I always say that if the Norse had a Yin and Yang symbol it would be Ingwaz. The fertility of Mind, Body, and Spirit can only occur when both our left and right hemispheres, our masculine and feminine being, our incoming and outgoing energies are engaged fully and in balance. Ingwaz represents the corpus callosum or bridge of filaments that unifies our left and right hemispheres. It reminds us to see the whole picture as well as the details.

Ingwaz comes after Laguz, the lake, the mirror that reflects our other self back to us. I love how Ingwaz shows Gebo looking into the lake and seeing its reflection - two X stacked. It reminds us to see, acknowledge, and balance our "other gendered half." As Karl Jung explains in his psychology, each of us has a twin inside of us. A woman's male half is called the animus, a man's female half is called the anima. Within myth and folk tales there are stories to help us balance these male and female energies within ourselves. Most of the heroic Sagas are about the hero on a quest for glory whose journey leads to a female figure. Sometimes this figure is a frightening troll woman whose embraces the hero must allow, swallowing pride and pretense. Then suddenly the troll woman becomes a princess and offers a drinking horn of poetry and wisdom to the hero, completing his mission. Sometimes the anima is a sleeping Valkyrie or death maiden. The hero must leap through fire and other obstacles to reach her. But only when he submits to her does she reward him by teaching him runes and other wisdom.

Perhaps the story of the stolen hammer articulates this best. Thrym, the king of the giants, steals Thor's hammer. This hammer represents all of his masculine or yang powers to contain and control the giants and wild forces. Only if Freya agrees to marry Thrym will he agree to return the hammer. Of course this is an impossible request. So Thor, in order to recapture his masculinity, must dress as Freya in bridal costume. He must not speak and must suffer the humiliation of playing this feminine role. Thrym asks for the hammer to be placed on the lap of his "bride" and Thor regains his power. This is an ordeal, an initiation of the most ancient sort.

Ingwaz is both inhalation and exhalation. The shape is also two kenaz runes, like Jera, but instead of whirling around one another, they come together - one opening out and one closing in. This shape is made in Scandinavian couple's dances as the partners step into one another, between legs, arms holding one another at the shoulder and back. It is the turn, the spin, the two create a whirling vortex that is balanced and very powerful.

Ingwaz asks, what is the other side of the story? It tells us to look for the duality in all things and, at the same time, to look for the unity. This rune brings things and people together to co-create, to establish fertile partnerships. Finally, Ingwaz can be used in manifestation. As a twin rune it doubles my luck, doubles my crops, and doubles my joy!

23. Dagaz

Dagaz, Daeg, Dag: phoneme d - day "God dag" is good day in Norwegian. Dagaz looks like a bow tie. It is an X, the rune Gebo (gift) with the two ends corralled by straight lines, which are the rune Isa (ice). Dagaz, day, is a gift of the sun for a short time. The day comes out of the ice of darkness and gives us heat and light in which to work, play, and interact with our surroundings before the ice time of night comes again. Dagaz reminds us to make the best use of this precious time. Our ancestors would have had complete darkness at the end of the day, especially in the winter. Just the hearth fire, the candle, the lantern, or the torch would light the way. In fact, it is Kenaz, ken, (<) to know, that we open up to in dream time then focus on during the day. Then we open up to Isa again. This is the process that creates the X within Dagaz' shape.

In Norse tradition, day, like sun, is given the essence of a sacred being. Day is Dagr, whose father, Delling (Bright One), guards the Door of Dawn through which Sunna (Sigel rune) must pass. He rides his horse Skinfaxi (shining mane) who snorts and shakes the dew onto to ground. Sunna rides after him with her two horse chariot. After Sunna, her brother Mani may wander up into the sky. Then comes Nott (Night) on her horse Hrimfaxi (frost mane). In some stories Nott is Dagr's mother. In some stories she is his grandmother and Jord (earth) is his mother. These images go deep into the Scandinavian Bronze Age (2000 BCE) in artifacts such as the Trundholm Sun Chariot. Dagr, Sunna and Jord are all depicted as runes attesting to their antiquity, importance and endurance as teachers of time, space, and life process for humanity in the Northlands.

Nott is inherent in the Dagaz rune as the ancient Norse count sundown as the beginning of the new day. The cycle, like the rune, begins with the icy flick of Hrimfaxi's mane, dark and sleep. Nott is responsible for impressing dream images into us. She is the daughter of the giant Narfi. Day cannot begin until the sun goes down. The full cycle is Nott, Dagr, Sunna, Mani - this is the triumphant procession of the celestial beings and an example of the balance of male and female energies so important to Nordic people.

Think how productive a day might be if we begin it as the sun goes down, dream fresh dreams, and then wake to fulfill them. We sleep, we wake, we do, we wind down and then we sleep again. A day is a cycle beginning and ending with sleep. We work hard during the day because we are assured of rest time. Isa, the time of quiet, slow movement and rest is at the head and foot of Dagaz. We need good rest in twice the dose as our hard work. Modern culture serves up quite the opposite idea. Too much awake time and not enough dream time!

The success of your day depends upon the quality of your dream time. Dagaz rune might be asking you to remember and work with your dreams. Dreamwork has always been a valued skill in folk culture around the world, inspiring art, music, and other cultural expression. The oldest known tune in Scandinavia was written down in runes on the back of a leaflet in the Codex Runicus (circa 1300).

"Drømde mik en drøm i nat um silki ok ærlik pæl"
It dreamed me a dream in Night of silk and finest furs.

In fact, we spend one third of our lives sleeping with the potential of 100,000 dreams in a life time. The value of dreams and dream work cannot be over emphasized as modern humans are generally sleep and dream-deprived. It is in the dream time that we may cross over into other worlds from Midgard. In dreams our disr (deified female ancestors) may come to help, teach and guide us. We receive so much information about awake-time in the dream-time it's no wonder Dagaz starts and ends with Isa!

Sleep deprivation is the source of so much illness in our modern world. Depression is not the least of these issues. Depression keeps people from even seeing the apex of Dagaz in Sunna, the life giver. Nordic people know about depression and Vitamin D deficiency from lack of sun. They have encoded the remedy into the runes. Keep your dream time regular, drug free, pitch black so your pineal gland will work again! There is too much light pollution, too much fake sun, interrupting the pineal gland and making good sleep difficult.

Your body, mind and spirit will know when it's time to slow down. Humans have a natural bio-rhythmic clock built to be highly sensitive to their particular environments. Small family group and tribal culture allows for member to self-regulate and members tend to regulate as a group quite naturally. Mani, Sunna's moon god brother, helps calculate the biorhythms, tides, ebbs and flows of energy in your body and across the subtle body of the Earth mother, Jord (Jera rune).

Modern Industrial culture is set on a specific clock that may or may not line up with personal or global cycles and bio-rhythms. Hourly and weekly business cycles do not generally change to accommodate personal moon cycles or bio-rhythmic fluctuations, or even the weather. Modern culture regulates group behavior mechanically, systematically and hierarchically rather than through the bio-feedback mechanism of equilibrium. Top down regulation and conformity has mechanic efficiency. But as a Nordic farmer type, I have never been able to get the hang of it!

Modern culture also stresses that when we feel our peak alert hours decline we should artificially stimulate them to continue with energy drinks, drugs etc. Sometimes there are reasons to push your day to the max, reasons and seasons for it, such as haying season. Farmers would extend their Dagaz energy with extra meals and power naps as my grandfather used to do. We can do yoga and other things for energy. Dagaz wants us to "make hay while the sun shines," but not force ourselves into fabricated light settings to maintain productivity. It is disrespectful to Sunna and Mani. Know when it's time to quit.

Not to sound like a mother, but everyone has to stop working and turn off the lights now. Unplug and let the night music of Mani's flute lull you. Look into the reflection of the lake at all you have accomplished. Have you done your best? Then you can rest easily. If you have not done your best then you must assure yourself that as Scarlet O'Hara said in *Gone With The Wind*, "...tomorrow is another day." Don't beat yourself up if you didn't accomplish all your tasks in a single day. That's another Modern culture thing to do – it asks us to feel bad about ourselves because we didn't accomplish the whole list of 45 things.

Dagaz says you shouldn't have a big list anyhow, or Gifu gets wonky and turns into Naudiz. The day's work categories are Mind, Body and Spirit. We must exercise all aspects of self in a Dagaz cycle. Dagaz is a cycle. It will always be a cycle. And if you start your day well rested with good dreams, those four things you do will be simply beautiful as they will resonate in Mind, Body and Spirit and throughout the Nine Worlds. Your work will be Ansuz powerful, simple, and divine.

How we feel about ourselves sets the tone for the next sleep cycle. Our emotions affect how we will sleep and dream. This determines the quality of energy our day will have. Respect the gift of yet another day to be alive; the promise of another day is our connection to the divine. We can show gratitude for this gift by caring for it and using it well. Being certain that Sunna will come again makes us grateful. Minds, bodies and spirits that are tired from just the right sort of work in just the right sort of proportions sleep well.

24. Othila

Othila, Othala, Othel: phoneme oh - heritage, homeland, inheritance. The last rune in the Futhark alphabet (though sometimes Dagaz and Othila are switched), Othila ends us and begins us. We reach the homeland only to start our journey all over again. Othila's shape is like Gifu, the X rune, with Kenaz on the top like a cone hat. The enlightenment of knowing (Kenaz) tops Gifu bringing us a deeper awareness of our relationships and gifts. It is the bottom or "root half" of the Ingwaz rune, the part that roots our fertility in our heritage. Othila can also mean our chosen family or aett, those to whom we are bound through adoption, marriage, and oath.

If there were a catch phrase for this rune it would be "Know thyself." People who have "near death" experiences often claim to have seen their entire lives pass before their eyes. It is a life changing experience. Sometimes people who "hit rock bottom" experience a death of their old selves as a transformation occurs. These are often referred to as shamanic deaths and they change and transform who we are in dramatic ways. Self exploration creates "little deaths" of our old understandings. To deeply understand ourselves, we must explore our roots, our genetic inheritance, our family and tribal "karma" or öorlog. Othila is öorlog.

The process of Othila is questioning and review. What did I plan to do with my life and what have I done thus far? Where do my attitudes, habits, and traditions come from? Did I learn them from my parents or grandparents? Did I inherit my worldview from the culture in which I live (which, in America, can mean the television or social media)? How are these cultural ideals different from those of my ancestors? Which traditions, habits, and ideals feel right to me and feed who I want to become? Do I have a family history of high blood pressure, cancer, addiction? These are important questions we must ask as we make choices for our lives.

Nordic people believe in a kind of reincarnation through the öorlog. You can be born back into your family line. If a baby died they would often call the next baby by the same name with the belief that the first had returned. This is the basis for a traditional first name that runs through the generations. The importance of family roots is intense as are our commitments to our families of choice, aett.

Though the Vikings traveled the world, when they died they often had their bones transported back to the places they were born. If this was not possible, the surviving family would sometimes carve a rune marker in the homeland in honor of the deceased. Family cemeteries are kept clean, visited frequently, and the dead are honored with flowers, gifts or libations and prayer-like conversations. Ancestor worship and family altars abound in every continent. Many cultures believe that after death the soul visits all the places it visited in life. These ghostly travelers have to gather the lessons of this earth walk in order to move to the next life. People often feel the presence of a deceased loved one in the places they held dear in life. Family altars keep people in touch with their deceased relations and provide doorways for such visits. This is part of the process of Othila.

Every way you look at it, creating a good life is the same thing as creating a good death, and subsequently, another good life. Death is the sum total of life. So what is the next life in Norse tradition? What is the ultimate "homeland?" There are nine worlds in Norse cosmology and the halls of your ancestors are in one of them. Most everyone has to walk the "Helroad," the path through Hela's hall where the dead are sorted. Depending on how this life was lived, what "shild" you still owe at your death, you could go straight to the halls of your ancestors and be reborn into your own lineage or you may stay trapped in a special place for oath breakers. Those who died of disease or by accident, without distinction, could be found in Eljudnir, the hall of the goddess Hel in Niffleheim. It was a place of feasting as well, cold but not uncomfortable and with access to the other worlds in case one was sent to run an errand. Such errands could be directives from Hel or other deities of the nine worlds. Dedicants of a particular deity may wind up serving them in their halls once they depart from Midgard. There are many deities, many halls, many worlds. The under-sea goddess, Ran and her nine daughters keep the drown men they find in the halls beneath the waves.

The only ones to escape the Helroad are those who die in battle and are taken by Valkyries (choice maidens) to either Sessrúmnir, Freya's hall, or to Odin's banquet in Valhalla where they can recount the stories of their exploits forever and practice for the great war, Ragnarok. There were two warrior halls because there were two different warrior initiation pathways. One dedicated to Freya and one to Odin. For a warrior, dying any other way than in battle meant shame and disgrace. There is a tale of an old warrior who was outliving his strength. He tied his gold and treasure around his neck hoping that someone would try to steal it. If he could die battling to defend it then he would join his friends in Valhalla.

Humans who had married Huldre or other underground creatures might be brought to live with their immortal lovers in Alfheim or other worlds. Our afterlife home is so connected to our lives here on Earth that even the Danish national anthem calls Denmark Freya's Hall! Othila allows us to align other worlds to this one as we search for our true homeland.

Used magically, the Othila rune can bring us safely out of trance, spirit journey, or astral projection back into the world our bodies occupy. Those who journey or gandreið (ride the wand) through the nine worlds may develop relationships throughout the worlds and be welcomed after death in the same way they were welcomed in life.

The Futhark is set up to lead us to the homeland in the best possible way. If we follow the lessons of the runes from beginning to end we have done the process of Othila. The 23 preceding runes shape us, jolt us, and make us who we are. The tapestry of our lives begins with the warp and weft of our ancestor's stories. From this we spin our unique strands, changing the patterns and adding new colors. But the weave has no end; it moves seamlessly into the tales of our children, nieces and nephews, the children of our cousins, neighbors, and friends. Our stories and those of our ancestors must be shared before we pass into the land of the dead because that is the process of Othila. That is how we find our homeland.

"Redwood Runes" photo by Kari Tauring, Oakland, CA, April 2016

Hiking in the Redwoods is hiking in the Runes. Every tree expresses every rune. We have but to see them, know them, and absorb them.

Runes in Divination

Divination is a word brought into Middle English from Medieval Latin, and therefore not a word that would have been used by early Nordic people. As a transitive verb first used in the 14th century it means to discover by intuition or insight or inference, to discover or locate (as water or minerals underground) usually by means of a divining rod. There is a long history of using a branch, rod, or wand (tein in Norwegian) to find objects underground, especially running water, mineral and gem deposits for mining, and lost objects. My grandfather was the "well-finder" of Polk County, Wisconsin. I know a few other elders who practiced this form of divination. On-line dictionaries give a huge list of ways to prophesy and their particular names. Some of them such as watching the flights of birds and horse snorts and stamps have been recorded in the Eddas, Sagas and other historical material.

The word for prophesy in Norwegian is *spå*. Prophet women are called spåkjærring. There is a lovely little song in one of the Norges Melodier (Norwegian song collections) called Desse Gamle Kjærringa (These Old Ladies). In it the singer proclaims that they can spå with coffee grounds, potato skins, and the stirrings of their pipes. Potatoes, coffee, and tobacco are post-Columbus or "new world" substances for use in spå. My grandmother told me that if I peeled an apple in an unbroken spiral I could throw it over my shoulder and it would give me the initial of the man I would marry. I can imagine that this was done by young girls in the ancient North as well.

Divination based on reading the signs of external tools and can be practiced by anyone who knows the formulae, ie. birds flying south is a good (or bad) omen. Were runes one of the tools used? There is a brief mention in Tacitus about priests who would cut slips of fruit wood and score symbols on them, casting them on a white cloth to aid in making decisions. This is from his Germani, circa 95 AD and written through second hand accounts of the people who lived near the Rhine. There is no way to know if the symbols were runes or not, or whether the idea of "casting runes" for divination was part of the culture. This description specifies a "priestly caste" and certain ritual for the process, definitely more than flipping a coin or rolling the dice.

As an intransitive verb, to practice divination is connected with intuitive perception. Divination as a noun is the practice of attempting to foretell future events or discover hidden knowledge by occult or supernatural means. It is perception by intuition; instinctive foresight. It relates to receiving knowledge from a divine source such as gods, land vættir, and ancestors. Creating a state of mind open to this sort of intuition through spinning, weaving and churning were well documented and so common that the Christian church in the 1600's wrote laws against women singing songs and charms while doing this sort of work. In the Eddas and Sagas, völur (staff carrying women) prophesied with the use of song and chant in ceremony and *seidr* (a trance-like state). They could speak directly to nature beings, the dead, and even to the gods themselves.

We do know that runes hold magical potency and were etched on sword hilts to improve the accuracy of the weapon or protect the user. They were carved into distaffs and spindle whorls to claim ownership and improve the quality of the spinning. Runes were sung in poetic forms for healing or aid in birthing, to bind enemies, and to detect/protect against poisoning. But we have no real evidence that they were carved on disks and used, like Tarot cards, in spreads or castings to predict the future. Historically, we do not know if runes were ever used in divination. They are certainly used this way in today's world.

More about spå

In this modern world, people come for "psychic readings" having the idea that we live on a time-line with a dead past, a volatile present moment, and a future that is somehow set in stone and able to be accurately foretold by an adept. The Sagas and other myths and legends written after Christianization carry many "Greek" concepts such as fate, destiny, and oracle. But this is not the way the world was understood in 95 AD by the Old Norse mind that did not have a future tense. Spå is about knowing and understanding historical precedence and reading the signs and energies that surround us now to predict potential outcomes or what "aught" to happen next. It is about achieving a state of *seid,* a heightened consciousness that allows the practitioner to see the invisible threads of the web of *wyrd* that connect past occurrence with what is happening now and continuing the weave in a way that creates a continuum of past to now.

Wyrd is a cognate of Urd, the first norn mentioned by the volva in the Voluspå. Urd translates to "is", historical precedence, öorlog, and everything that has already been done. The past, in a Nordic mindset, is vibrant and alive, constantly informing our present moment. The past is being continually created through the power of the second norn, Verdandi, becoming. The third sister is Skuld whose name means debt and should. Skuld is also a Valkyrie (choice woman) and the norns are called "*nauthigastir*," guests of need. They appear at the time of our birth and death along with other disr (deified females). These are times of most compelling need where human life hangs in the balance. So spå depends upon historical wisdom, localized environmental wisdom, and accurately reading the signs that present themselves in order to advise on what, by necessity, ought to happen next.

My History as a Rune Reader

In the Havamal, Odin asks these questions of the would-be rune user:

> dost know how to write, dost know how to read,
> dost know how to paint, dost know how to prove,
> dost know how to ask, dost know how to offer,
> dost know how to send, dost know how to spend

All of these questions Odin poses have an underlying question - have you done your studying?

I first began studying the runes in 1988. First I wrote them on a wall chart and memorized them. Then, I created a rune set by painting the runes on oak plugs made by my father. I carried each rune for many days before making the next one. In this way I could "live with it" and see how it related to my life during the time I carried it. After about a year of studying and growing my relationship with the runes, I began to use them for "readings" for friends and family. It became my standard birthday gift. This practice gave me the experience of learning how the runes relate to and are affected by one another. Early on I used a basic three rune "past, present, future" layout. In coming to understand the principals of the ancient mindset, I began drawing a rune for each of the Norns which illuminates the history, describes the moment, and advises on the the course of action one should take. I also experimented with more Tarot-style lay outs.

In the early 2000's, I read at fairs and farmers markets. The most affective training for me was doing quick, two minute, one-rune pulls at High School Graduation "lock-in" parties. This forced me to intuit which stories about the one rune most fit with the person who drew it. It also revealed the patterns within the group consciousness. In 90 to 100 readings each night, certain runes would repeat themselves and in this way I got a feel for the group consciousness of the particular graduating class.

I have used runes is in translating people's names into runes and then "reading" the name. Constructing a poem from the flow of each rune always seems to depict the client's personality so accurately. With this method, however, you need to decide whether to spell the name phonetically or letter-for-letter, keeping in mind that some letters are not present in the FUTHARK. This takes some practice and conversation with the person whose name you will translate and read.

My method for spå

I get into a light seid state by aligning with the world tree. I ground into the three roots and pull the energy of the three wells up my spine and into my head. This is fully explained in the Volva Stav Manual (2010, lulu.com). Very often I will do a little spinning on my drop spindle to illustrate the principals of the norns, call them to help, and get into the proper mindset. I ask my client to align with the world tree as well. I give them the basket of runes and ask them to clarify their question and get their energy into the runes as they do so. Clearing energy out of the runes is easy when using wood runes in a basket as shaking them and mixing them both clears the prior person's energy and infuses them with the new person's energy. Usually by the time people are aligned and clear about their issue, they intuit the answers immediately themselves. I ask them to draw a rune (or however many are required). Then I read/interpret/tell stories about the rune(s) they chose which generally serves to verify what they themselves already know. Sometimes clients need to talk about what their real questions are before they shake the basket.

Questions

Yes and No - to me, runes are not the best tool for yes and no. Pendulums and flipping coins are better. Runes tell us what energy is flowing through one direction or the other. You could pick one rune for yes and one for no to see what energy each choice has surrounding it. Alternatively, decide that a reversal will mean no and see which way the rune comes up.

There are some questions that are very strange to answer in the context of runes and the lack of future tense. Many people want to know what their future will be like. How many children? When will I find a mate? These are rather awkward questions for runes to answer in my experience. Again, a counting method such as pendulum might be better suited to answer these things. A practical, utilitarian Nordic will answer the question of how many children you will have by asking the question, do you have a mate? You can choose a rune to see what the energy is surrounding the question of children, but that is often unsatisfying to someone who believes in a set and unchangeable future.

If I am starting a new project I may pick a single rune to illuminate the energy of the project or pick one rune for each of the team members to see how we will all work together. If choosing between two jobs, pick one rune for each choice. If someone is in transition and looking for general guidance, I will have them choose a rune for each norn, Urd, Verdandi and Skuld. This is a good way to approach a birthday reading as it gives a glimpse into the energies that are forming. It is a good reading to use on the solstice and equinoxes as well. Using the runes to balance male/female energy in the body can be achieved by drawing one in each hand. Then I read the lessons for each rune as it pertains to energy balancing. They can be carried as amulets to remind the client of the balancing process. A daily/weekly rune can be used as a meditation, to set the tone of the day or warn of obstacles that might appear during the course of things.

Reversals - To me reversals are not always negative or dark portents. They often ask whether you are looking at the branches or the roots? Are you looking into a mirror? What are you projecting and what is reflecting back to you? Reversals can be very helpful in determining the course of action. As an example, a man came for a reading who was obsessed with a woman he could not have. I asked him to pick a rune for himself and he got Ehwaz the Horse. The rune he picked for the woman was Laguz the Lake, reversed. Basically I told him, "you can lead your horse to her water but you can't make her give you a drink!" Reversals often just remind us not to avoid the lessons of that rune.

Cursing and causing harm with runes - is a very bad idea. I do not go in for anything like that so if that's your aim you will have to find another author to support you. It is a simple adage but a true one, whatever you send out returns to you three fold.

Rune Sets

First of all, there is no evidence that people carried around a bag of runes the way we do these days. Many books describe elaborate rituals, Ceremonial Magic and lots of "hoopala" to create sacred runic tools. Tacitus' description specified fruit wood and white cloths. In a post-Christian world where the sacred and mundane have been divorced, it may well be that people require extensive ritual to bond in a sacred way with objects they consider mundane. However, in the pre-Christian mindset, there is no separation of sacred and mundane. The very act of relationship creates a sacred bond and even "mundane tools" such as spindles and swords were given names and passed along in families. For this reason, the best tools are the ones we make ourselves or inherit as this creates deep relationship.

Secondly, our first relationship must be with the runes themselves, not with the wood or paper or clay we inscribe them on. For this reason I advocate using slips of paper to make flash cards. You could wood burn some popsicle sticks. Get some stones and paint them. I make sets from the Buckthorn trees being eliminated throughout Minneapolis as an invasive species. When I prune my trees and find a few lovely long branches, I make stavs, teins, and rune sets out of them for friends and family. This gives the tree respect and a new sacred life.

While Nordics are a utilitarian folk with little time or good weather for extra ceremony, we understand the sacredness of nature. Runes, remember, are the secret whisperings of nature. They exist everywhere in our environment and if we are present in our environment they will surface like familiar faces to encourage us, warn us, or to set us straight on our journey here on Earth.

Nordics are very education oriented. As you memorize and internalize the shapes, sounds, names and meanings of the runes you can go outside, close your eyes, formulate your question, then open your eyes and read the runes in your environment. Every rune can be found in a single tree, in sidewalk cracks, and in the way your silverware spills into the sink for washing. The power of the runes is in your relationship with them.

Runes and Runos

What was it that Odin "grasped" as he hung on the world tree? Scriptural rune shapes and meanings or poems and incantations, the other meaning of rune? Magical poems abound in Nordic literature from the rune poems Groa taught to her son in Groagaldr and the runos chanted by Väinämöinen in the Finnish National Epic, Kalevala. During the early Iron Age there was a good deal of sharing between the Indo-European and Finno-Ugric tribes. Both the scriptural runes and poetic runos share the Sanskrit root word ru (secret or whispered mystery). Runos are a particular style of poem with eight syllable lines, alliteration, and often they have line repetition. The first song on my recording "Völva Songs" (2008) is a runo in the nearly extinct Uralic language, Votic. A women's bridal ritual for the sauna, it describes the magic properties of the waters used in such ceremony.

Galdr is a form of magical song, galdrlag is the poetic formula for this. When someone says they are "galdring runes" I ask if they are following the Old Norse poetic "magic spell meter" with a fourth line variation of the third and special attention to alliteration. Usually they mean that they are toning or howling out rune names. Singing the runes names is a very powerful experience but I prefer to call it rune chant to eliminate confusion. Sounding a rune with the addition of creating the rune shape with the posture of the body is a highly effective way to learn, incorporate the energy of, and potentially send the energy of runes.

Galdr is related to a word "galen" which means frenzy. Odin was the god of frenzy and ecstatic states as well as poetry and magic. So this term fits with many aspects of rune use. Poetry, word play, and kennings (nick-names) are essential parts of Norse esoterica. The idea of writing and reciting poetry for healing has been beautifully explored by Yves Kodratoff in his book, "Nordic Magic Healing: Healing Galdr, Healing Runes." Remember that everything in Norse tradition is about relationships. The healer's relationship to the disease begins with finding out the name, source, and lineage of the disease. Creating a poem to compel the disease out of the patient is only as powerful and effective as the relationship the healer has with the disease, just as a love poem is more powerful when one has someone in mind. Using rune script within the context of the healing poem, hypnotic chant meter, alliteration, rhyme, kennings and repetition are essential to the healer, the disease, and the patient.

Bind Runes and Other Uses

Finally, we come to the use of runes for which there is abundant evidence: writing them on objects. They have been used in combinations for marking boundaries, in tattoo designs, for banners, grave markings and general graffiti. Grave or memorial stones are the most common finds and often contain proper names as the subject as well as the name of the author.

Bindrunes refer to a combination of two or more runes twined in a design. Often people will use their first and last name initials. Working with your name is a safe place to start. These are letters you have lived with all your life. The letters that make up your name are deeply embedded in your mind, body and soul. Family names are carried through the öorlog. Translating a family name into runes and creating patterns and bindrunes with the letters can be a powerful way of connecting with ancestor energy.

What I recommend to most people who ask my advice about using runes is the same advice I give for those wanting to use them in divination. Get to know them intimately. Feel how they work in your life energetically. Be certain about your intention. Follow the advice Odin gives: know how to write them, read them, paint them and prove them, ask them to help, make an offering to the gods, send the energy out with good will and complete the circuit of energy, the Gifu of the relationship.

Glossary

Aesir – Meaning simply "gods," Aesir is the name of one clan of deities in Scandinavian Mythology originating with the three brothers Odin (spirit), Vili (will) and Ve (holiness). Their mother was Bestla, a Jotun who sprung from Ymir. Their father was, Bor, the son of Buri, the first "hero" licked free of the ice at the beginning of creation by Audhumla, the cosmic cow. This trilogy killed Ymir and created worlds from his body. The Aesir built a walled fortress to live in (Aesgard). They had visitors from the Vanir clan of deities who were nature magical, shape shifters, and versed in the arts of seidr and spae. An envoy of the Vanir, Gulveig (gold might), came into their camp. They pierced her with spears and burned her three times, though she came out of the fire more shining and beautiful each time. The Vanir demanded weregild (payment for murder) and Odin chose to begin a war instead. The gods were evenly matched so to put an end to this un-winnable war they exchanged hostages to live as guests each other's halls. The Aesir had strict taboos against sibling marriage and placed the great value on the manly qualities of battle. Njord the Vanir sea god and his twin children Freya (Lady) and Freyr (Lord) came to live with the Aesir. Nerthus (the presumed sister of Njord) fades out of the popular mythology. Freyr marries a Jotun female and they reign over Alfheim, elves world, and agricultural pursuits. Freya teaches Vanir magic to Odin and becomes the most important goddess in the Norse pantheon, though in post-Christian writings she was minimized to being a goddess of love and sex.

The post-Christian attributes of the Aesir are probably more patriarchal and hierarchical than they actually were depicted in the pre-Christian world of Heathens. Snori Sturluson (author of the Prose Edda) wanted to connect the Aesir and Odin to the Greek heros of Troy. While in Indo-European language the Greeks are cousins of the Germanics, it seems unlikely that there is a direct correlation to be made. The characters of the Aesir mythos can as easily be likened to the Hindu and Vedic characters and mythologies.

Aett – 1. Old Norse for clan or aett was a social group based on common descent or the formal acceptance into the group at a Ting, the Scandinavian version of a pow wow. 2. In folk tradition, an aett is also a set of eight runes that make up a family of runes relating to one another. Freya and Freyr's Aett is the first eight runes in the Futhark, Hel or Heimdal's Aett, is the second eight, and Tiza or Tyr's Aett is the final eight runes in the 24 Elder Futhark.

Audhumla – This is the name Scandinavian mythology gave to the cosmic cow that wandered the icy plains in the earliest moments of creation. Ymir, the giant, drank Audhumla's milk, and Audhumla licked free the first "hero" of the Aesir, Buri, who was trapped in the ice. The concept of the sacred cow traveled with the Indo-European migration including Aditi and the great Goa in East Indian traditions, Hathor in Egyptian myth. Cows were sacred throughout the Celtic and Germanic world and are the subject of rock art dating into the European Ice Age (20,000 BCE).

Brigid – Celtic goddess of the triple fire: hearth, smith craft, and poetic inspiration whose altar flame was guarded by 13 priestesses. She relates to the rune Ken and to Naudiz, the need fire. Sainted by the Catholic Church, 13 nuns guard her sanctuary in Ireland today.

Brisingamen – The magical necklace of gold and amber belonging to Freya. When she saw that Loki had tricked the Dwarves into making presents for Freyr and some of the other gods, Freya took herself directly went to the Dwarves demanding a present for herself. The price she paid for the work of four dwarves was to spend one night with each of them. (There are also four dwarves who hold up the four corners of the world who are named after the four directions). There are several wonderful re-tellings of this story on the internet and elsewhere. It is a classic tale of innocent female energy moving into the dark or shadow side and coming out more powerful as a result of the journey. The necklace represents Freya's ability to transcend darkness and ordeal to take her rightful place as the daughter of Nerthus, queen of the Earth.

Joseph Campbell – researched and wrote about the similarities in mythologies around the world. *The Hero with a Thousand Faces* was his most popular work. Check out the Bill Moyer's interviews with Joseph Campbell. They are very inspiring.

Celtic Calendar – Sometimes called the "old agricultural calendar" the Celtic calendar follows the astronomical events of the Equinoxes, Solstices, and the points in between, creating eight distinct holy periods. The Nordic calendar generally splits the seasons into three seasons but with winter solstice (Jul) and summer solstice (mid-Sommar) being the highlights. From the beginning of time, humans have pondered and celebrated these times of the year. Ancient astronomy and astrology has monuments to the significance of these points in the year. The Pyramids of Egypt, the Granges and Henges of Europe, and the Pyramids of Teotihuacan near Mexico City are just a few examples. The 8 spokes of seasonal change have been important to agrarian societies from the Neanderthal to the *Old Farmers Almanac*!

Chakra – Means "wheel" in Sanskrit. The human body is like a battery with negative and positive energy flows. At certain points along the spine and joints, the energy rotates. There are seven chakras along the spine in the "Kundalini" energy system beginning at the base of the spine and moving to the crown of the head. Each chakra point carries the colors of the spectrum as follows (base to crown) Red, orange, yellow, green, blue, indigo, and violet. The base chakra is red, the wheel turns slowly, and it releases energy related to survival, instinct, and Earth based needs. As the energy travels up the spine, each wheel turns slightly faster giving off a different color and relating to issues less material until the crown chakra, as violet, relating to enlightenment and healing energy.

I include this in the book for several reasons. First, our Nordic ancestors would have had some understanding of these concepts as our common Indo-European heritage contains many similarities between Vedic or Hindu gods, concepts, and artistic representations. Second, the concepts of the spine as the trunk of the world tree and the chakras as worlds circling this tree are ancient and used in shamanic practice throughout the world. Third, in describing how the order of the Futhark flows as a life path and a road map to enlightenment, I see the similarities to the lessons of the chakras and how different runes relate to the chakras. Lastly, our global community is becoming so unified that finding the "truths" of all systems and sharing this information seems imperative for the advancement of our human condition.

Crone – The three acknowledged stages of the female being are **maiden**, youthful, innocent and free, the first crescent of the moon. Her menstrual cycle and burgeoning sexuality create the melting snows of spring time, often personified in Scandinavia as Idunna or young Freya and in Germany as Ostara or Eostre after whom Easter was named. The **mother** aspect is the educated, understanding, and disciplined aspect of the female psyche and the full moon. She uses her menstrual blood to grow other beings. Her time is summer and autumn, when growth is ripe and nourishing. We picture her seated with a cornucopia on her lap, flowing out to the people. Frigg and the mother aspect of Freya are pictured here. The **crone** is the aspect of the feminine that is done with things of the Earth and the waning moon. Her menses have stopped and she "keeps her wise blood to herself." Winter is her time, the dream time and the introversion. She is free of the responsibilities of motherhood like the maiden but not care free. Wise and without restrictions she can travel safely between the worlds. Here we picture the aged Pertcha or Holle. Norse tradition offers a look into the fourth face of the goddess cycle with Hel. She is the transition from Crone to Maiden again, the dark face of the moon and the great mystery of re-birth.

Crow's Law – In Jamie Sam's book *Animal Medicine*, Crow knows and understands the laws of the universe. The phrase, "as the crow flies" regards the actual distance and direction from point A to point B. For a human walking this distance there may be rivers and mountains in the path causing the distance and direction to shift. But for crow, there is a bigger picture. And the bigger picture overrides the individual concept of reality. Crow's law is *öorlog* in ancient Norse understanding. It is the natural law that says, despite our efforts to command, we must in the end obey. In many interpretations, the **Norns** are responsible for tracking and in some cases influencing a person's *öorlog*. They write down the primal laws.

Eastern Medicine – Homeopathic-based medical treatments. The assumption in Eastern or Chinese medicine is that symptoms occur to alert us to a root cause. By treating sinus inflammation with more of the same, the symptom is pushed into running its course more quickly, thereby revealing the underlying cause. Eastern medicine treats the human body as a whole, organic organism whose parts are intimately connected. Each organ, for example, has a relationship to pressure points in the feet, hands and head and is connected to emotional states and the environment (including seasons and times of day).

Masaru Emoto – Japanese researcher whose studies about how thought and emotion affect water became a global sensation. His book *The Hidden Messages in Water* shows photos of frozen water that has been subjected to different environments. Water that had been exposed to messages of hate and water exposed to messages of love was then frozen and observed under a microscope. The water exposed to hate messages barely formed crystals while the water that had been loved had exquisite crystal structures. [Note: a piece I wrote, The Journey, about Mimir's well – the well of a Norse god known for his wisdom – was performed as the opening ceremony for a conference in which Emoto was a key note speaker.]

Eve and Adam – The primary story of Adam and Eve comes from the book of Genesis in the Hebrew Bible (see Hebrew Bible). The book tells two creation stories. In one, God creates man and woman from dust. The myth of Lilith, Adam's first wife, is part of this version of the story (see Lilith). The second creation story tells us that God put Adam into a deep sleep and took a rib from his chest to create the female, making woman a "second generation" creation and subject to man. The name Eve means Mother of Life.

Adam and Eve's original residence, the Garden of Eden, was a land of plenty, but one without much going on. Challenging Eve's concept of truth, a "serpent" tells her that if she eats of the tree of the knowledge of good and evil she won't die as God had told her she would. Tempted, she eats and receives the understanding of good and evil, by which she procures free will for humanity. She gives the fruit to Adam, and both are expelled from the garden into the world where their free will is to be forever tested and their choice-making is to be wholly their own. This story represents the transition from being fed all we need from above to needing to create what we need through human relationships. It is the beginning of **Mannaz**, which brings us closer to divine nature (as the angels in the garden feared would happen) as it makes us creative rather than simply receptive beings.

Feng Shui – Meaning literally wind and water, Feng Shui is the practice of observing and manipulating the environment to better serve the flow of chi or energy through a room, a garden, or even a person. Coming originally from China, Feng Shui astrology is linked to the I Ching, a system of divination and numerology. In Chinese philosophy Feng Shui is one fifth of what creates the total human ordeal. Destiny, luck, Feng Shui, education and philanthropy are the five points that humans must understand and pursue in order to gain completion and enlightenment. In Norse tradition, the web of wyrd that connects individual öorlog carries an energy much like wind and water. The völur were adept at manipulating the elements, people's thoughts and energy through seidr.

Fenrir – The wolf, son of Loki and Angrboda, Fenrir will aid in the destruction of the world. He is bound by a magical chain that the gods slipped on him through trickery. The god Tyr agreed to hold his hand in Fenrir's mouth as a trust measure while the gods bound the wolf. Tyr lost his hand in the bargain, paying "shild" for breaking his trust oath with Fenris.

Fire Rune – Many people try to relate each rune with an associated color, tree, element, deity etc. While they all come from the natural world and relate to the elements of nature, some runes lend themselves to more obvious associations. Runes such as Naudiz, Kenaz, and sometimes Uruz, have associations with fire. Runes such as Isa, Hagal, Laguz, and Ansuz relate to the element of water. The runes of the trees are Berkanan and Ehwaz. They may also be called earth runes along with Jera, Othel, and perhaps Algiz. There is only intuition when it comes to making these associations and one should feel free to relate any rune to any element they deem appropriate to the work at hand. Strict rules of association should be held as highly suspect.

Freya and Freyr – The twin deities of the Vanir whose names mean Lady and Lord respectively. Ing and Ingvi are another set of twin deities who may indeed be equivalent to Freya and Freyr. Freyr is often called IngviFreyr. As in other cultures, the concept of the female and male twin gods is common in Scandinavian myth, especially when it comes to the Vanir. Many scholars see Nerthus (the Bronze Age Earth Mother) and Njord (the god of the sea) whose names are cognate as the brother/sister twin parents of Freya and Freyr. This kind of mythology relates to human psychology and brain development. Each human has a male and female side, the left and right brain, the yin and yang, the positive and negative charge of our energy flow. By destroying this concept in mythology, humans have allowed one side to dominate, the masculine side. This shows up in all sorts of dysfunctions as subtle as punishing left handed children (the right or female side of the brain controls the left side of the body), creating entire educational systems that teach only to left-brain linear thinking, or dysfunctions as obvious as the oppression of women. [Freya and the Vanir have been linked back to the earliest migration out of the Indus Valley through stories of the Huldre (fairy women connected with Freya) being the children of Lilith, the first wife of Adam who left the Garden of Eden when she refused to submit to the male. This is part of Norwegian folklore even up into the early 1900s.]

Frigg – Frigg (meaning beloved) represents women's transformative arts like spinning, weaving, and child birth. She is a prophet and owns a shape shifting falcon cloak as Freya does. She is married to Odin and took Odin's brothers as her consorts when he was away for several years, emphasizing her role as Queen and the symbol of life, fertility, and potential king-making. Some authorities think of her as an aspect of Freya or even as Nerthus. She is the one who "knows all and says nothing," which leads me to think that perhaps she is Nerthus of the Vanir, come to legitimize the Aesir's rule and aid in raising her twins.

The Elder Futhark – (or **Older Futhark**, **Old Futhark**) is the oldest form of the runic alphabet used by Germanic tribes for Proto-Norse and other Germanic dialects of the 2nd to 7th centuries A.D. for inscriptions on artifacts (jewelry, amulets, tools, weapons) and for use in alphabet magic, poetry magic and possibly divination. The Elder Futhark contains 24 runes, each having individual sounds and meanings. The Younger Futhork (the O indicating a linguistic shift in the letter Ansuz to Os - both meaning mouth) contains 16 rune shapes. Anglo Saxon runes and other variants were devised in the 1300's.

Outlawed as pagan and replaced by the Roman letter alphabet, much of the meaning and lore of the runes was hidden in secret societies and folklore. In the 1600's, rune masters suffered the fate of witches and were burned and tortured. (Many had their tongues cut out.)

Giants – In Old Norse, Jotun. Before the Aesir gods were "born," there were giants in the world. The first giant is Ymir (meaning howler or groaner) was created through the connection of ice and fire. Anyone who has had a cauldron fire out on the ice while fishing has heard this sound and has seen how frosty fingers seem to grow from the ice and ache towards the fire. Ymir was a hermaphrodite, like an amoeba, able to create from his/her self. Stories describe Ymir as slow and sleepy, like a giant baby. Sucking from the world cow (see Audhumla) he slept and sweated other beings, other giants. Giants could shape shift, had magic, and could mate with other species. Odin's mother was the giant, Bestla and Ymir would have been Odin's maternal grandfather/grandmother. Odin's father was Bor, son of Buri who was licked out of the ice by Audhumla.

Some stories say Ymir was jealous of Buri's good looks and noble bearing and so started a war against him and his clan. Other stories say that Ymir was so unintelligent that the three sons of Bor, Odin, Vili, and Ve began to fight with him. Another possible cause for war with Ymir may even be his hermaphroditism. Odin's clan, especially in post-Christian writing, is notoriously patriarchal, anti-feminist, and intolerant of marriage with close relations. Ironically, Odin finds that to achieve his goal to be an All-Father, he must learn women's mysteries (see Odin), a full karmic cycle. Another way to think about this myth is that Ymir is the chaotic, constant creative force of sound. The three brothers as Spirit, Will, and Holiness, divided chaotic sound into music, creating the worlds from his/her body, the sky from his/her brains, the sea from his/her blood, the blood was so immense that it flooded Ganungagap and nearly drowned all of the giants. During the flood, a frost giant named Bergalmir saved as many of his people as he could. They washed up in a tree trunk on the back of Ymir, now called Jotunheim, the new land of the giants. In circular fashion, Ymir creates, is destroyed, is created from, and so on.

The Aesir are victorious against the giants and the Vanir (see Vanir) gods. But, alas, their karma will come full circle when Surt the Black, leader of the fire giants, avenges Ymir at the end of the world. He will call the other giants together, slaying the Aesir and some of the Vanir, as all the worlds of Yggdrasil (see Yggdrasil) end in flame. That is the time called Ragnarok (see Ragnarok). Of course, out of the ashes of the old will come the new as the prophecy of the völva (see Seidr) predicts.

The Hebrew Bible – the Torah or Pentateuch, first five books of this Bible. In these stories, Abraham and his descendants form the basis of the three major "Abrahamic" religious traditions, Judaism, Christianity, and Islam. All three share features such as patriarchal monotheism, legalism, and strong traditions of community and social service. These traditions are part of the Indo-European language root and must be considered in the deep öorlog of European peoples.

Hopi – The Hopi are indigenous to the southwest of the United States of America. One creation story tells about how a thought became a thread for the spider to begin weaving the world. Thought Woman and Spider Woman are sometimes different entities, sometimes interchangeable. I recommend the book *Being and Vibration* by Joseph Rael to more fully understand Hopi spirituality and especially the relationship of sound to creation. In Norse tradition it is the Norns who spin the web of wyrd that connects reality, time and space.

Heimdal – The son of nine Jotun women, guards the rainbow bridge Bifrost (quavering sound) between Midgard (our human home) and Aesgard (the home of the gods). He came to humanity three times, engendering the gifts of culture. He went first to the house of Great Grandmother and Great Grandfather who represented Thralls, peasants and a slave personality. He infused them with his divine nature by co-fathering children among his hosts. He repeated his "grace" by visiting the Grandmother and Grandfather, Karls, free men and women of industry. Finally he came to Mother and Father, Jarls who have achieved gentry. Like the figure of Jesus, Heimdal gives the gift of divinity to all of humanity. His visit raises them from their prior condition. While some use this tale to support the three class system (upper, middle, lower), I see Heimdal imparting his unconditional love and gifts of the gods to all people. I see these as the names of epochs rather than classes. When the Giant Surt comes to make war at Ragnarok, Heimdal will blow the Gjallarhorn (resounding/yelling horn) to alert the nine worlds that the time of reckoning has come (see Ragnarok). This horn is also used by Odin's maternal great uncle Mimir (meaning memory or pondering) to drink from his wellspring Mimirsbrunner. One of Heimdal's nine mothers is Gjalp, the giantess who confronted Thor at the sacred river Vimur. The underworld river is called the Gjall and the bridge between the world of the living and the world of the dead is called the Gjallarbru. As usual in Norse tradition, name similarities and associations are indicative of relationship.

Hel – One of Loki's children by Angrboda, giantess Queen of the Ironwood. Hel is half maiden half crone (see crone), ruler of the underworld where all souls not taken directly by Odin or Freya's Valkyrie are bound to go. Those lost by accident can be lost on the icy plains of Nifhel. Oath breakers, according to some stories, have an especially nasty place in Hel's halls. Musphel is the fiery side of the underworld that straddles Ganungagap at the roots of the World Tree. In Norse tradition the underworld stands in balance with the middle and upper worlds of the tree as all of the deep Indo-European root traditions believe.

In modern Christianity, the concept of heaven and hell as either/or places to go upon death, seems quite opposed to both the Nordic belief and to the Hebrew concept of Sheol (land of the dead) which is where everyone goes after death in that tradition. Sheol is more similar to the Finnish concept of Tunolo, ruled by a god/goddess pairings and the Baltic gods of the dead, Velna (wizard) and Ragana (witch), both staff carriers. I find it interesting that Norse tradition separates the god/goddess pairing and puts Hel the crone/maiden in the underworld where Christianity places a dominating male deity, the Devil. The bridge to Aesgard is regulated by Heimdal, a male deity with nine mothers. (The Christian heaven is regulated by a male deity as well. Jeshua was born of a Hebrew mother, Mary. There were two other significant Mary's in his life. The Magdalene and his mother's cousin. All three were present at his death and resurrection in the New Testament stories.

As stated above, most people pass through Hel's hall and then proceed to the halls of their ancestors where they may be reborn into their ancestral lineage, following and completing strands of öorlog within the web of wyrd of their heritage. Norse texts (written in a post-Christian time) tell of an especially horrible place in Hel's domain for oath breakers and other heinous humans. Valkyries (death maidens or wish maidens) stem from the Norn Skuld and Freya's lineage of disr (deified women). They can take favored heroes, völur, and special favorites of specific gods directly to their halls. Chosen warriors of Odin who die in battle may be taken directly to Valhalla in Aesgard and Freya's battle slain join her Sessrumnir (many seats in Folkvanger "the valley of the folk"). Frigg, Saga, Thor, Freyr...all of the gods have their own homes among the nine worlds and may collect souls to their homes as they desire.

Baldur, who lost his life to Loki's cruel trick, has rooms in Hel's hall, Eljudnir where he must stay until Ragnarok, the end of the Odin cycle and the beginning of a new öorlog for the Aesir. Even powerful Frigg, Baldur's mother, cannot retrieve him from Eljudnir.

Mengloth (glad drink) has a hall built by nine dwarves on the mountain Lyfjaberg (medicine mountain) sometimes placed within Hel's realm as it is surrounded by a fiery fence as Eljudnir is. Hel's bed is called Kor, "sick bed." Also a daughter of Jotun lineage, Mengloth has nine disr who surround her and serve her cause of healing (including Eir, who also serves Frigg and the Aesir as a healer). She is surrounded by other numerological and ancestral lineage of significance.

Huldre – In Scandinavian mythology there are many sorts of creatures that are not quite human. They are referred to as the "unseen folk", the "little people" or sometimes collectively referred to as "tusse-folk" even today. Farm and house helper "folk" were Tomte (Sweden), Nisse (Norway), and Tonttu (Finland). Trolls of rock and wood abound outside of the farm enclosure. Water spirits like nykken (shore line), fossegrimin (waterfall), and others were important to appease for good fishing, safe water passage, and even to help learn nature music and magical songs. The huldre (males are huldu) lived underground and in the woods but sometimes married into humanity, and lured or stole humans to live with them. They looked like beautiful humans but with a cow tail (sometimes fox tail in Sweden). In huldre eventyr (huldre folk stories) and huldre stille (huldre tunes) they are credited with teaching human women how to herd, churn butter, keep clean houses, and sometimes to spin and weave. In "The origin of the Huldre Folk: The Huldre Minister" Collected by J. Skar in *Gamalt fra Setesdal* (1903), all the tusse-folk are described as the offspring of Lilith, Adam's first wife and his equal in every way. They left the Garden of Eden freely and are therefore without sin. Therefore, as the Huldre tells the minister, none of the tusse-folk need the New Testament (see Lilith).

Indus Valley – The flood plain region of northern India to the "fertile crescent" between the Tigris and Euphrates rivers in modern day Iraq to the Anatolian peninsula. The Indo-European language family is tied together by common origination in this area, home to one of the first known "sedentary" cultures. Weather changes causing flooding and drought and population expansion caused a clash between Aryan-Iranian nomadic culture and the settled agricultural communities of the Indus Valley resulting in the Indo-European migrations. Sanskrit is the Indo-Aryan liturgical, poetic, sacred language of the Vedas, kept holy to this day in India. The root word ru - in runes and runos comes from Sanskrit. Nordic cosmology, metaphysics, and poetic content have some roots in the Vedas.

Journeyman – One who goes "on the road" with his or her craft, especially in regard to bards or musicians. This is a person in mid-career who must go through the trials of creating fame for him or herself in the wide world. This is the step before becoming a Master in your craft.

Carl Jung – A student of Sigmund Freud, Carl Jung advanced the theories of dream analysis. Jung promoted the idea of individual human psychological makeup and dream characters as archetypes found within mythology. These archetypes live within the collective unconscious minds of individuals, cultures, and all of humanity. Jung used active visualization to create interactions between the dream characters and the ego of the dreamer in hopes that the characters would integrate with the dreamer, creating a healthier, more whole individual.

Karma and Dharma – Karma is the law of cause and effect stating that the actions you do return to you. A deep part of Hindu and Vedic teachings, most every culture has some related concept to karma.

128

Even in physics we say that every action has an equal and opposite reaction. Karma is the accumulated return of actions from myriad lifetimes whereas dharma is related to the destiny of this particular incarnation. As we work to maintain a balanced life devoid of emotional attachment, karma and dharma become neutralized and enlightenment is attained. There is also a strong tradition of appeasing ancestors and deities to change karma. In Old Norse, this would be wyrd and öorlog respectively though not corresponding exactly.

Lady of the Lake – Female deities (disr) have always been related to bodies of water. In India the river Ganges bears the name of Ganga, mother goddess, and is believed to *be* her materially as well. In Greek and Roman mythology, the water nymphs and spirits often provide magical weapons to heroes, and sirens of water lead them astray. In Celtic lands, the lake goddess is called either Nimue or Vivian. In Bronze Age Scandinavia, the cart of Nerthus the Earth Mother was driven into a lake to be ceremonially bathed. Those who assisted the goddess appear to have been drowned in the same lake after bathing her. Water is yin, or female, receptive and absorbing, dark and slow. The lake is the womb of woman, the center of life. The river is the flow of menstrual blood, the essence of creation.

Lilith – In Hebrew and Babylonian folk mythology Lilith was described as Adam's first wife (correlating to the vague first creation story in Genesis – see Eve and Adam). They were both created from the dust at the same time and Lilith considered herself equal to Adam in every way. She refused to be submissive (most tales relate this to sexuality) which frustrated Adam. Adam complained to God, and Lilith left the Garden of Eden in a huff. God sent angels to retrieve her but she refused to come back. As the tales develop Lilith is called a screech owl and a demon that preys on children and men in their sleep. Descriptions of her, conjure up associations with Athena, her winged cap and owl totem as well as with Freya who dons a feather cape and is free with her sexuality and magical potency. Lilith is further linked to Freya through Norwegian folktales of the Huldre (see Huldre).

Loki – Loki is one of the most complex characters in Norse Mythology. He was of the race of giants who became Odin's foster brother. He represents everything about human sexuality that the

Aesir despise. As a shapeshifter he took the form of a female animal and birthed Odin's eight legged horse, Sleipner. He had liaisons with many creatures most notably Angrboda, the giantess. From this union came Fenris (or Fenrir), the wolf who will slay Odin at Ragnarok, Jörmungandr the sea serpent who will aid in the destruction of the world, and Hel, who rules the underworld that keeps the hero Baldur. Loki keeps the Aesir off balance causing the strife out of which the gods attain their gifts and a higher state of being. Some scholars link his name to fire. As Odin's sworn brother, he can live in inngard, but only with caution, as like fire, he must be maintained diligently. In one tale he travels with Thor to the house of Utgard Loki, the face of all elements whom Thor is unable to conquer. In post-Christian teachings, Loki is likened to the devil and his name is not allowed to be spoken or referred to in some Heathen groups. In other Heathen groups, he is considered more like Saturn, the god who makes us confront our öorlog head on and either learn our lessons or suffer and perish.

Medicine Wheel – From The Wheel of Law, adapted from the work of Joan Halifax by Robin Van Doren, 1988. My teacher encouraged us to learn the directional characters of the wheel while honoring similar characters from our own cultural heritage. I have found these positions on the wheel to relate to brain physiology as well. These are the basic descriptions as they were given to me along with my notes relating these characters to Celtic and Nordic archetypes as well as the Celtic (agricultural) calendar. I find it interesting how the male and female energies are balanced around the wheel of the year and with one another. The same holds true in Norse tradition. Keeping in mind that all of these "characters" exist within each of us, it is possible to do this exercise as a solitary.

We enter the circle through the North East - The Pattern Keepers - The gate keepers are Male then Female. I think of them as I do the Spider Woman of Hopi tradition and the Norns of Norse tradition. The Pattern Keepers' job is to keep the integrity of the circle throughout the ritual. They see the *gestalt* – the whole, the web of wyrd for the Norse. They are the web weavers, the fates, the ones whose permission is needed and whose final word is law. These people are intuitive, can sense energy shifts, sensing truth and worthiness. If they allow it, questioner enters the circle and proceeds East.

1. East - The Fools - Two Male Energies
Other names for this character are Coyote, Loki (in Nordic tradition), trickster, the adversary. The quick wit of the rising sun, the mirror back on ourselves. Idea hatcher, lover of jolly good fun, the new moon. Causes friction so we can learn something. Spring Equinox. The seeker asks their question to the east and is given a question in response. The "real" question, so to speak. And this is what they take around the circle to the rest of the stations.

2. South East - Tradition - Female then Male Energy
Tradition sits next to the Fool. This is the character within us that holds knowledge of the way things have always been done. Tradition answers the seeker's Fool's question from the standpoint of history. This position gives us the framework, the boundaries, the reference points and the lessons learned from the past. May Eve or Beltane on the wheel of the year. Saga is the goddess with whom Odin drinks each morning, to learn the lessons of history. She lives in a sunken hall beneath the waterfall of time and space.

3. South - The Warriors - Female then Male Energies
The attributes of the South are personified in the warrior. The heat of passion, the heart center, the noontime sun, Summer. The full Moon. The Warrior is the character of action and has the special function of protecting the children's fire in the center of the circle. The Mother protecting her children. No thought of hesitation, only feeling. The Warrior will answer the question from this place of the heart and with the sacred duties in heart. Summer Solstice. **Center** – While the questioner does not go to the center it is important to know that the Grandparents (who are the past) sit on either side of the children (who are the future) at the fire in the center of the circle. The children's fire must never be allowed to die or be threatened in any way. This way we protect the past and the future. Valkyries are compelled to come only twice in a person's life, at birth and death. This is a warrior principal.

4. South West - The Shaman - Female then Male Energies
Facing the Pattern Keeper, a shaman is nothing without a community

to serve. The shamans are the healers, the interpreters of dreams, the keepers of the faith. They rely on the Pattern Keepers for balance and grounding when they are in their states of ecstasy. They will answer the questioner with psychic insight mixed with the health of the community and the individual in their thoughts. Spae folk and some more community oriented völur (staff carriers) may fill this role in Norse communities. Gothi or gythia can also fill this role. Lughnasadh, the first harvest.

5. **West - The Witches** - Two Female Energies
The Crone, the waning moon, wise woman, she doesn't care about community per se. Like the Fool opposite her, she is only interested in her own knowledge. She is in control of the Magick, the dreamtime, the setting sun, the autumn time. She will sacrifice the grain god with no remorse. She is sexuality and operates out of the sensual where the Fool operates out of the intellectual. Fall Equinox. Völur and vitkis (staff carrier women and wise men) were the witches of the Northlands. Under Freya's teaching, Odin attained the skills of the staff women and was chided for it by Loki and called ergi (unmanly).

6. **North West - The Tribal Chiefs** - Male then Female Energies
Sitting across from Tradition, the Tribal Chiefs weigh the information and give answers/make decisions for the general workings of the Tribe. Where we will hunt in the fall? When we will travel in the spring? Will we make war or peace? The tribal chiefs are the diplomats in this great circle of opposites and strong personalities! They are gathering information, listening hard. While the Shaman is concerned with the individual as part of the whole and the pattern keeper is concerned with the whole as part of the universal, the Tribal Chief sits opposite Tradition who has knowledge of the history of the whole and makes decisions about what the whole might be. Samhain, Halloween, the sacrifice of
the King. In Norse tradition, chieftains would take the advice of the völva very seriously in weighing options.

7. **North - The Creators** - Male then Female Energies
The first Thought Woman, the Logos, the sun when it has set, no moon, winter and the dark secret knowledge of creation, the void womb before conception. The Creator answers questions from the logical and scientific. The Creator can answer the why's of things

because she creates everything. The Creator sits opposite the Warrior, whose passion and heat are like the woman giving birth. North is the conception. Winter Solstice. Ymir is the creative sound force in Norse tradition and Odin, Vili and Ve are the logic and ordering principal of creation.

8. North East - the Pattern Keeper - Male then Female Energies Addressed at the end of the ritual, the Pattern Keeper decides whether the participants were truly speaking from their archetypal character or answering out of personal opinion. If the integrity of the wheel has been upheld, the seeker is free to depart and ponder the answers given by the archetypes. Imbolc, the blessing of the seeds to start the process again.

Moon Gods – the following are some examples: **Mani** in Norse myth, **Khons** and later **Toth** in Egypt, **Sin and Nanna** (twin lovers) in Summerian myth, **Soma** in Hindu tradition, **Tsuki-Yomi** in Japan, **Tezcatlipoca** in Aztec culture and even **Allah** in the pre-Islamic Arab world was a moon god with three powerful daughters, one of whom was his equal, named **Allat.**

Mjolnir – the name of Thor's hammer. Accurate and final in its blow, it acts like a boomerang and comes back to him each time he throws it. Made with an error (due to Loki's interference) by the dwarves, the hammer has a too-short handle and requires an iron belt and glove to complete the electrical circuit seen as lightening. (See Thor).

The Nine Worlds – In the beginning was the void. **Ginnungagap**, is the gaping void of creation in Norse tradition. **Niflheim**, the world of ice and frost comes into contact with **Muspellheim**, the world of fire. These polarities combine to create the field of salt and brine on which we find Ymir the giant and Audhumla the cow. The nine worlds are re-created by the three brothers out of Ymir's body as his blood flowing destroys the first worlds created in Ginnungagap. Snorri and other writers try to put the nine worlds in relationship to one another on the "world tree" best known by the name Yggdrasil. In my spå (prophesy) I have found that the worlds and wells align with the body, with the spine as the trunk of the tree. I will give them here.

The three lower worlds are **Niflheim**, **Muspellheim** and **Helheim** - Ice, Fire, and in-between - left foot root, right foot root, perineum root. The three wells correspond with Urdsbrunnir, Mimirsbrunnir and Hvergalmir respectively. The three middle worlds are Midgard (human home - heart center), Ljosalfheim (above ground elves home), Svartalfheim (underground elves home)*. The three upper worlds are Jotunheim (giants home) located in the occipital ridge, Vanaheim (Vanir's home) - the right brain, and Aesgard (Aesir's home) - the left brain. The High Seat is the pineal gland (consult my Völva Stav Manual for more details).

*The idea of light and dark elves is a post-Christian notion posited by Snorri. The worlds would be Alfheim and Nidavallir the world of elves and the world of dwarves.

Here is an excerpt of a chant ritual to take a group of people to Mimirsbrunnir, a way of pondering the meaning of the world's waters.

Norns – The most significant concept you must understand about the Nordic mindset is that there is no future tense. So the Norns do not weave the future per se. Urd means "is". She represents the historical content of all the world's öorlog. As with the rune Uruz, she is primal. Nordic's look constantly at past precedence, lineage, and origin and the relationships within the past. These relationships determine the potential of the moment. Verthandi is "becoming". She holds the point between the spun and un-spun stuff of the universe. She does not let go of the moment until Skuld shows what by necessity ought to exist. Skuld is the last Norn and the first Valkyerie. Her name translates to should, necessity, and is the root of shild or debt.

They spin öorlog and the web of wyrd, the weave or pattern of inter-connected lives that present "fate patterns" of potential and probable outcomes for humans and gods alike. Völur are adept at sensing and often manipulating these wyrd lines. The Norns are ancient female beings who live by the well-spring named for Urd, Urdsbrunner. The cosmic tree is the cosmos and the three sisters are the rune users who keep the cosmic balance in alignment. It is through the three Norns that we really start to understand the astrological, cosmological, and metaphysical nature of what the runes are all about.

Odin – Odin is a very complex character. Called Wotan or Wod in German, Odin means spirit, breath or inspiration. The first poem in the elder Edda (Grandmother) is the Voluspa, the prophecy of the staff carrying woman, where the seer basically reads Odin's öorlog. She tells Odin's history from creation, to the burning of Gullveig, to the sacrifice of his eye for a drink from the Gjallarhorn at Mimir's well. He is a definite "sky god" with Frigg representing the "earth goddess" and the mother of Baldur. His famous son Thor was the result of his relationship with Jord, who is literally the Earth. Odin has offspring from other female beings as well. There is evidence that Tyr and even Thor, were earlier forms of the sky god, but Odin developed in the stories, hearts and minds of the pre-Christian Germanic and Scandinavian into a fully realized living god.

In literature he evolves as a deity from High, to More High, to Most High. As the eldest brother of the sons of Buri, son of Bor he sacrificed/killed the giant Ymir and created worlds from his body and humans from an ash and an elm washed up on the shoreline of the new world. Odin was a renowned warrior god and chief of the Aesir. Driven by the desire to be the All Father, seeking all manner of wisdom he gave his eye for a drink out of the well of wisdom. He emasculated himself, learning women's magic from Freya, joining the völur in ritual. He caused himself to bleed as males must do*, in order to understand the nature of the runes while hanging in sacrifice from the branches of the world tree. From this episode we get the name Yggdrasil (the terrible one's steed). Ultimately, however, as the Voluspa tells us, Odin's time must come to an end. Ragnarok is the predicted outcome of his öorlog, the necessary end of the old world tree and the beginning of the new order wherein his son Baldur will be released from Hel's hall and reign over a time of peace and plenty.

In Rudolf Steiner's Theosophical interpretation, Odin is breath, sound, word. Thor is blood, will, ego. Freyr is imaginative intelligence. In the body, Odin is one pulse to Thor's four beats. In staving, Odin is the stav pulse while Thor is the tein beat. Odin is the air, the breath to the beat of the heart blood of ruddy red Thor. Together they allow the Freyr/Gerda (spirit/body) connection to evolve.

Odin is associated with the singing of galdr (poetry in galdrlag or magical rhythm) to create a state of galen (frenzy) which is also associated with the heights of ecstasy achieved in dance, trance, and war. The Berserkers (bear shirt warriors) were dedicated to Odin and used alcohol and psychotropic mushrooms to create an out-of-body frenzied state in battle. Unfortunately, these warriors were extremely cruel and perpetrated atrocities on whoever was in their way.

*Women bleed freely each month and gain wisdom through the womb's blood. There are countless heroes and gods who must hang on the tree of life, pierced in the side, and bleed freely in order to achieve the enlightenment of their female half.

Psyche and Cupid – from the Greek Myths, Psyche was a human woman with whom Cupid, the god of love, fell in love. Cupid asked Psyche to stay blindfolded and remain in the dark about what he looked like because he wanted her to love him purely and didn't want his godly visage to affect her. She agreed and was quite happy until her sisters convinced her that he might be a monster. She broke the vow, took off her blindfold and lit a torch. Seeing the god of love next to her, she caused such a start that he woke up. The vow broken, Cupid fled, but his mother, Venus, wanted the couple to be happy so she raised the status of Psyche to demigoddess and she lived with Cupid from then on. This myth has been the subject of much feminist critique. It echoes the story of Adam and Eve, a fall by female curiosity with the evolution of consciousness as the result. It echoes the story of Freya who goes into the underworld to seek the Brisingamen necklace from the Dwarves and rises up more powerful than ever. It is the story of moving from blissful ignorance to the tragedy of discovery, then to the evolution of consciousness that allows us to come closer to our divine nature.

Poetic Edda – or the Elder Edda (Edda means grandmother) is a collection of poems written in Icelandic around the 1270's A.D. by anonymous authors from oral tradition. They were found in the Codex Regius in the 1600's.

Prose Edda – Called the Younger Edda by its author, Snorri Sturluson (1179-1241), the prose Edda is a manual for would-be poets. It contains lists of kennings (like nick-names) for the characters and places of the world tree, alternative stories, cosmologies, and gives insight into the pre-Christian/post-Christian transition of the Nordic mind set.

Ragnarok - The war to end the world. Ragnarok will be preceded by a three year Ice Age, heralded by three cock crows and the blowing of the Gjallerhorn (see giants and wellsprings). The war is foretold by the seidrkona (see Seidr) or sybil in the Voluspa Edda (see Voluspa). Ragnarok is the culmination of Odin's öorlog, possibly brought down upon Odin for his long list of mis-deeds. In this final war that destroys the worlds of the Aesir (see Aesir), crushes the Bifrost Bridge, and burns the world tree (see Yggdrasil), many of the beloved gods meet their end. But as with all endings in mythology, and indeed in things scientific as well, endings are merely beginnings of a new thing. After the war, Baldur will be released from Hel's halls to reign in the new world. The two humans saved in the trunk of the tree by Mimir will re-populate the new world. The cycle of life and death and re-birth will begin again.

Reincarnation – Unlike the Hindu concept that you can be reborn as a dog or tree, Norse tradition teaches that we can be reborn into our öorlog. We are our ancestor spirits come back among the living by being re-born into the family line. In Scandinavia, the practice of naming a new baby after one who had recently died or after a grand or great-grand parent whom the baby resembled was related to this ancient notion. This tradition continued into the Immigrant Era in Minnesota and is still held to in Iceland where naming babies has legal rules around it.

Rune Poems – There are four central rune poems, mnemonic devices that preserve and even somewhat obscure the meanings of the runes. Since rune magic was outlawed by Christianity at the time the Rune Poems were written the authors would have been writing through the filters of Christian ethic complete with all the cultural baggage it brought with it. Modern readers may pull meaning from these texts through our own experience with the concepts presented. The four main rune poems are the **Icelandic Rune Poem**, the **Anglo Saxon Rune Poem**, the **Norwegian Rune Poem**, and the **Abecedarium Nordmannicum**. www.northvegr.org/lore/main.php#indo is an excellent resource for reading all source material on runes and Norse mythology.

Sabbat - This term is used in modern Wicca and other neo-paganisms to mean holy days that fall on the Celtic agricultural calendar. The word may derive from the Jewish word Shabbat (meaning resting point). Modern Heathenry does not use this word or the Celtic and Roman calendar dates for the seasonal festivals but there are enough similarities that inclusion of it seems important. The following dates are the "generally accepted" dates for the solar festivals and their mid-point festivals. I will start with the Heathen equivalent and expand to the Celtic, Christian, and secular holidays that surround it where appropriate.

1. October 30 - Winter Nights and the Wild Hunt when Odin, Freya, Frau Holda and the hounds of Hel ride the earth collecting the souls of the weak and unlucky. It is the start of hunting season and the culling of the herds. It marks the beginning of the Juletid (Yule) Winter season and the Celtic New Year. Called Day of the Dead (*dia de los muertos*), All Saint's Eve, and Halloween.

2. December 20 Winter Solstice - Mother Night, a special moment during Juletid when the night lasts longest and the sun is weakest. Sunna, the sun goddess, finally gets to stay home. All spinning must be completed by this time as Frau Holda or Frigg, patron goddess of spinners, comes to check everyone's work. All wheels must stop turning so as not to disturb Sunna's rest. In Latvia, they still use a wagon wheel as decoration for winter solstice, placing a candle on each spoke (later creating an advent wreath of them). All cultures have a "coming of the light" celebration in Mid-winter, though dates vary widely: Hanukkah in Jewish traditions, Diwali in Hindu tradition, Christmas in Christian tradition, and Kwanza in African-American tradition, and Ramadan in Islamic tradition.

3. February 2 - Charming of the Plow, calling on the goddesses and often Freyr to begin stirring the light elves to wake up. Imbolc, meaning ewe's milk, when the lambs are born and the milk starts to flow, St. Brighid's Day, Groundhog's Day, purification of Mary, seed sorting time, the original end date of winter and the beginning of spring.

4. March 20 Vernal Equinox - Eostre/Ostara, the Germanic goddess of Spring, Easter. In Norway the tradition is to go on an Easter ski. In Sweden and parts of Finland they have preserved the "Easter Witch" where young girls and boys dress as witches with rosy cheeks and head scarfs. Going door to door with their pail they collect sweets and give blessings with birch twigs.

5. May 1 - Walpurgis Nacht after Walburga the Summer goddess in Germanic tradition, Beltaine or May Day, assumption of Mary, enlightenment of Buddha and the beginning of Summer, chickens lose their winter feathers (great for hats), workers' holiday.

6. June 20 Summer Solstice - Midsommersdag, again, spinning stops while Sunna rests and the wheels are taken off the wagons, only this time, they are lit ablaze and rolled down the mountainsides. It is also Thingtide, beginning the season of travel to festivals for selling wares, trading livestock, and joining in the Thing meetings (legal gatherings). Litha, the height of the Sun's power.

7. August 2 - Freyblot or Loaf fest, celebrating the first harvest of the grain. Lughnasaad, John Barleycorn's Day and the end of summer holidays as the farm work begins to speed up.

8. September 20 - Fall Fest or Harvest Fest, if the grain is all in, the threshing dances are done at this time. Lammas, the fruit harvest, Bacchus' Festival, Fall Cleaning.

Saga - Saga is a giant goddess whose sunken hall is beneath the waterfall of time and space. Odin comes to her every morning to drink her wisdom. The sagas are a series of heroic tales from which countless ballads were sung and danced (and still are today). These tales almost always contain a hero who must submit to the female power in order to complete his mission, gain a drink from their wisdom horns, and often achieve a marriage or union with deified females in this way.

Sami – Once referred to as "Laplanders," the Sami are the indigenous population of Scandinavia whose culture is based on following the herds of reindeer. They moved into the extreme north first because the receding ice left a climate too warm for reindeer. They were moved further north by the cultures who came to farm the lush soil left by the receding ice. Another classic tale of the clash between sedentary agricultural people and ranging hunter/gathering society, the Sami still range with the herds of reindeer as much as possible, and new laws are making their way of life a little more supported. It is hard to say what parts of Sami tradition, language and culture influenced the new comers of the Bronze Age who brought their goats and sheep into Scandinavia from northern Iran, and vice versa. As Christianity gained influence over Scandinavia during the late Viking Era, Heathens were cruelly persecuted. After conversion, the oppressed became the oppressors and the traditions of the Sami were outlawed, drums were burned and shamans were tortured into forced conversions...it's an old cycle I hope we can break.

Seasonal Affective Disorder – S.A.D. As sunlight decreases in the winter time, most people feel the physical effects such as increased appetite, sluggishness, isolationism and irritation. These effects are countered by full spectrum light bulbs, increased intake of B-complex and C vitamins, and healthy, supportive interaction with community. Most of this can be accomplished through winter holiday traditions that have been handed down. Yet if these traditions go unobserved, have been distorted through commercialism, or if a person has a natural tendency towards depression or suicide, more drastic measures should be taken to combat this natural phenomenon.

Serenity Prayer – "God grant me the serenity to accept the things I cannot change, the courage to change the things I can, and the wisdom to know the difference." Used in the Alcoholics Anonymous tradition to release dysfunctional, controlling behavior.

Seidr – Seidr relates to a branch of Scandinavian women's spiritual practice connected to Freya. In my teaching I use Yngona Desmond's definition of "seidr as wyrd consciousness." It is a state of being whereby one can perceive the subtle energy of the web of wyrd and follow the strands into the öorlog of the "client" whether that be an individual or a community. In this state one can also communicate with land spirits, make prophecies (spae or spå), heal, direct elements of nature (such as wind and water currents) and sway the minds of people or groups (such as armies).

Central to attaining a seidr state is poetic song-chant and rhythm to induce a trance-like state during which the shaman's mouth would spring open and she would speak of past, present, and potential future events. The most adept at these arts were the völur (staff carriers) whose staffs were buried with them in rich grave sites. Spinning and seidr are connected in many stories throughout the Eddas and Sagas.

Sun Goddesses – the following are some examples: **Sunna** – Sometimes Summa, may date to the Scandinavian Bronze Age, associated with Nerthus. **Saule** – Sun goddess of Latvia and Lithuania. **Sekhmet** – The Egyptian sun goddess, Sekhmet represents the sun's more destructive side. She is called the eye of Ra. Ra is a less destructive sun god. **Cautha** – Etruscan sun goddess (circa. 5th Century BCE). **Kultepe** – Anatolia sun goddess (circa 7th Century BCE). **Amatersu** – Japanese sun goddess who hides in a cave and comes out at Winter Solstice. **Walu** – Australian aboriginal sun goddess. **Igaehindvo** – Cherokee sun goddess.

Thor – the son of Sky and Earth (Odin and Jord), his thunder wakes up the fields and his rain makes them ready for planting. He wields Mjolnir, the hammer that keeps the Frost and Fire giants in balance throughout Midgard. He is also a god who develops and grows over the course of the stories about him. He achieves maturity and balance first by realizing that Utgard Loki was unbeatable (the very essence of Nature Power) and by losing his hammer, only to regain it by assuming female form (submitting to the feminine divine). He became the most favorite god among pagans even into Christian times, representing the working man and the legal system. He deals out justice at the base of the world tree. The Hammer symbol was found in jewelry molds alongside the cross. (In Norway the cross was depicted as Gifu, with lines of equal lengths). Called Donnar in Germanic, Perkunas in Baltic, and Ukko of Finno-Ugric tradition. Finnish hammer necklaces and designs were very popular and similar to the Scandinavian ones. He is celebrated through the image of the julebukk or Christmas goat that hangs on the holiday trees of Scandinavians today. The tradition of going julebukking is also still practiced in some Norwegian-American enclaves here in Minnesota. Dressed in goat horns and furs, masked revelers go from door to door seeking alms for the poor and treats for their songs and dances.

Tiw and Tyr – Two names for the same deity in the Norse pantheon. Tyr means "god". The Prose Edda claims Tyr is the son of Odin, the Poetic Edda says he is the son of Hymr, a giant. Tacitus the Roman historian places him with his Earth Goddess consort, Ziza or Isis, as a tribal variation of Odin. His most important feat in the stories is having sacrificed his hand to calm the chaotic energy of Fenrir the wolf (see Fenrir).

Valhalla – (see Asgard) Death Hall, the hall of feasting for warriors who died in battle. The winged shield maidens, Valkyries, select half of the slain for Odin's hall, the other half belong to Freya.

Vanir – The clan of deities with whom the Aesir went to war. The rulers of the Van before the war were Njord, a god that rules the shoreline to the open sea. Etymology and speculation state that his sister/consort was Nerthus, goddess of the land who lives on an island in the middle of a sacred lake. These are obvious associations with water. Vann is water in Norwegian and while it may be more folk etymology, I associate Vanaheim with water. Njord and Nerthus children are the twin deities Freya and Freyr (Lady and Lord), who were part of the hostage exchange along with their father after the war. Freya remains forever connected to gold and amber (the golden resin that floats on the salty sea). She cries tears of gold and her daughter is Gnoss, the jewel. Both twins have sacred boars, associating them to the animal in other ways such as fertility, wealth and intelligence. The popularity of the two as fertility deities lasted well into the late Viking Age. One custom still practiced into the Immigrant Era was to bake a loaf in the shape of the julebor (jul pig). Some was eaten and some was saved until spring when part of it was given to the earth, part put into the grain storage areas and part was eaten by the workers before plowing the field. My family keeps this custom with my annual "pig cookies" - one of which is saved for the garden in the spring.

Archeology of the Scandinavia Bronze Age (2,000 B.C.E.) reveals gold-leaf sun discs, bronze horns in left and right pairings, and other beautiful metal work. Rock paintings and small statues of ceremonial male dancers with horned helmets and acrobatic women in string skirts are still visible in Scandinavia. My intuition is that the Vanir are the memory of this ancient culture that brought goats, sheep and pigs into Scandinavia for the first time. In the Eddas, the Vanir are creative and pro-creative with no taboos on sexuality. Their magic was nature spiritual and "shamanic" - shape shifting, weather working, and soul manipulative. Odin learned this magic from Freya.

Freyr is called Yngvi Frey, connecting him to another god/goddess pair - Ing and Invine. Tacitus and other writers comment on the prevalence of god/goddess pairings. Some say Ullr and Ulli are another such pair along with Tyr and Tzisa. It's possible. Twin deities who are siblings have a long historical root in Indo-European mythos. Njord will return to Vanaheim (and perhaps to Nerthus) after Ragnarok.

Viking – To go viking is to wander from home. It names the era during which the lands of Scandinavia could not sustain the burgeoning population. Around 10% of the population went off adventuring on longships. Vik also means "bay" and describes the little inlets along the shoreline of Scandinavia which their longships were so adept at navigating. Scholars believe that most of the Viking expeditions were financed by the wealthy land owning women for their younger sons who would not inherit the farm. They would "raid, trade, or settle" in the lands and populations they came across. From the early 700's to the mid 1000's AD, from the Celtic Isles to the Black Sea and east into Russia, men and women (and the cattle the women owned) invaded and settled, building new communities such as Dublin, York, and Kiev.

Völva - In Old Norse this translates to staff carrying woman (plural is völur). The first poem in the elder Edda is the Voluspa (prophecy of the staff carrying woman). These women were dedicated to the arts of seidr, spå, runes, healing, and other magical arts.

Wellsprings

1. There are three in Norse Mythology (see Nine Worlds). Hvergalmir, the bubbling cauldron, the source of 11 rivers that flow through the nine worlds is located in the gap between Niffleheim and Muspellheim. A great dragon, Nidgahog, guards this well. Mimirbrunner or Mimir's well, is situated at the root of Yggdrasil running through Jotunheim, home of the giants, is guarded by Mimir whose name means ponder, seeing, gaze and sometimes memory. The well water contains memory, knowledge, and wisdom. Odin is one of a few who dared to ride into Jotenheim and challenge Mimir for a drink of the well. Odin's eye still stares out of the bottom of that well. Such was the price for a drink. The third wellspring is Urdbrunner named for the Urd, the first of three Norns (see Norns). This well contains the historical record of all of life and each individual strand of öorlog.

2. In relationship to Tai Chi Chuan (martial arts coming from China) and Chinese medicine, each foot at the kidney chi point is a bubbling spring that connects to the earth body. The third root connects through the perineum, an important energy vortex in Eastern and East Indian esoteric work. Water is a central component in the Chinese system of Feng Shui (literally wind and water), the practice of arranging the environment to direct chi (energy) that flows through it (see Feng Shui).

Western Medical Model – Based on Allopathic medicine, the idea that treating symptoms by creating an opposite reaction has been the basis of Western medicine since medieval times. For example, one would treat inflamed and moist sinuses by shrinking and drying them out. Western treatments are meant to treat and relieve symptoms rather than the causes of disease. It looks at the human organism as separate parts rather than an organic whole which sometimes results in a treatment for one symptom causing difficulties in some other aspect of the system. For example, a pain reliever for arthritis may cause stress on the heart. Nordic healers work in a more homeopathic way with the whole system - body/mind/soul complex as well as within the inter-dimensional world tree, finding the source and lineage of the disease and thereby gaining power over it.

Yggdrasil – First introduced as mjötvið (wish tree) by the Volva, this cosmic world tree holds the inter-dimensional reality of the nine worlds together. The world tree, the tree of life, and reference to the human spine as a tree can be found in all Indo-European mythologies and around the globe. Yggdrasil is a kenning for the tree of life rather than the name itself. It translates as "Odin's horse" or "the terrible one's steed." This kenning comes from the story about how Odin accessed the runes by hanging himself for nine days, bleeding from his self-made wound. It seems reasonable to think he would have to hang one day for each of the nine worlds. Irminsul and Hod-Mimmirs Wood are among the other names for this tree. Broomsticks, distaffs, the "Hobby Horse," the Shamanic pole, the cross bar of the drum and the staff of the völva are tools of the "astral journey" practice and are metaphors for the world tree which we ride, like a horse, through the cosmos.

Yin and Yang – In Chinese philosophy, Yin and Yang are the dual aspects of all creation. Yin represents the dark, receptive, negative charge of the battery; it is female, the gestalt, and is right brained. Yang represents light, activity, positive charge, and things male, linear and left brained. The balance of these dynamic forces is seen in what is called the Tao. Yin and Yang is a universal concept in human understanding that opposite energies interact to create an altogether new dynamic. In Norse creation they are Ice and Fire, Vanir and Aesir, and the adherence to male/female pairings and dualities within the deity systems and the stories of the Saga heros.

Ymir – Meaning "howler" or "aching groan," this hermaphrodite giant appeared from the interaction of ice and fire at the beginning of creation. He fed from the udders of Audhumla, the cosmic cow. Ymir is the father/mother of other races, and the progenitor on the female side of the Aesir (see Giants).

"Journey to the Wells" photo by Jack Bartholomew

Kari took the entire audience on a journey to Mimir's Well to remember our deep connection to water, the source of life. The following is a revision of that original journey by Kari Tauring

"The Journey" – Tauring, 2004

Eagle, hawk and cock I see

perched up in the branches three

4 winds, journey deer, move across the crown

(Astri Vestri Sudri Nordri)

Ratatosk, journey squirrel, I am moving down

(chick chick chick chick chreeeee)

Nine worlds three wells the journey has begun

Nine worlds three wells breathe as we go down

1st Stage – Level One

Alfheim – Vannehiem – ancient elves and gods

Worlds, I see them, two of 9 across

Alfheim – Vannehiem – Freya bless my passing

Skirt the river Ifling

Midgard human home another of the 9

Asgard Odin's land bless me as I ride

Urdarbrunner first well, guarded by the Norns

Urdarbrunner well of fate Urd Verdhandi Skuld

(Urd, Verdandi, Skuld makes three, Wyrd sisters of Fate, Being and Necessity)

Ride away, ride away, North we go and all

(Rida Rida Rida Riii Nordri alle com mit mir)

2nd Stage – Level 3

Down and down and deeper still, to the Northern land we ride

Muspellheim the seeds of all, primordial the fiery tide

Niffelhiem and Hel's domain, water raging Hvergalmir

Worlds collide sparks and steam, the source of rivers flowing clean

Who guards the wellspring of creation? Nidgahogg the Water Dragon!

(Nidgahogg Ginnungagap – Austri Austri Rida vi, Austri Austri com mit mir)

3rd Stage – Level 2

East the path that Odin took, riding through the worlds again

To the world of Nidavelier, through the world of Svartalfheim

In Svartalfhiem the dark elves dwell but Jotunheim contains the well

Cross the river deadly cold, river Ifling never froze

(cross the Ifling deadly cold, river Ifling never froze)

Jotunheim the giant's land, rock and frost the bane of man

Down and down the root we go beneath the world the sacred well

Mimir guards the water there, Water Etin primordial!

Bibliography

I am indebted to these authors for their contributions to enlightenment. Reading and research is important. Yet, there is no substitute for living with the runes and recording our own traditions as we use them in our daily lives.

Allan, Tony. The Vikings: Life, Myth, and Art. New York: Barnes and Noble, 2004.

Anderson, Hans Christian. The Complete Hans Christian Andersen Fairy Tales. New York: Crown Publishers, 1981.

Asbjornsen and Moe. Folkeventyr. English edition. New York: Pantheon Press, 1982.

Aswynn, Freya. Northern Mysteries and Magic. St. Paul: Llewellyn, 1998.

Bear, Sun and Wind, Wabun. Medicine Wheel: Earth Astrology. New York: Fireside Press, 1980.

Barber, Elizabeth Wayland. Women's Work: The first 20,000 Years. New York: Norton and Co. 1994.

Barber, Elizabeth Wayland. Prehistoric Textiles. New Jersey: Princeton University Press. 1991.

Blaine, Jenny. Nine Worlds of Seidr Magic. London: Routledge, 2002.

Campbell, Joseph. Hero With a Thousand Faces and The Power of Myth. Princeton: Princeton University Press, 1972.

Capra, Fritjof. The Tao of Physics. New York: Random House, 1975.

Carlson, Laurie Winn. Cattle, An Informal Social History. Chicago: Ivan R. Dee, 2001.

Colton, Anne Ree. Watch Your Dreams. Glendale: Griffin Printing, 1973.

Condron, Barbara. Kundalini Rising. Windyville: School of Metaphysics Publishing, 1992.

Crossley-Holland, Kevin. The Norse Myths: Intro and Retelling. New York: Pantheon Press, 1980.

Davies, Brenda. The 7 Healing Chakras. Berkeley: Ulysses Press, 2000.

Desmond, Yngona. Völuspa - Seidr as Wyrd Consciousness. US: Booksurge, 2005.

Emoto, Masaru. The Hidden Messages in Water. Hillsboro: Beyond Words Publishing, 2004.

Gitlin-Emmer, Susan. Lady of the Northern Light. Freedom: Crossing Press, 1993.

Gårdbäck, Johannes. Trolldom: Spells and Methods of the Norse Folk Magic Tradition. Forestville: Yronwode Institution Press, 2015.

Haas, Elson M. Staying Healthy with the Seasons. Berkeley: Celestial Arts, 1981.

Haugen, Einar. Norsk Engelsk Ordbok. Oslo: University Press, 1967, 1974.

Hollander, Lee M. The Poetic Edda Translated. Austin: University of Texas Press, 1962.

Honko, Timonen, Branch, and Bosley. The Great Bear: A tThematic Anthology of Oral Poetry in the Finno-Ugrian Languages. Pieksämäki, 1993.

Jung, Carl. The Archetypes and the Collective Unconcious. (and other works)

Keary, A. and E. The Heroes of Asgard. New York: Mayflower Books, 1870.

Kodratoff, Yves. Nordic Magic Healing, Universal Publisher.com, 2003

Kvilhaug, Maria. Maiden with the Mead. VDM Verlog, 2009.

Mason, Antony. If You Were There: Viking Times. New York: Simon and Schuster, 1997.

Ornstein and Thompson. The Amazing Brain. Boston: Houghton Mifflin Co., 1984.

Paxon, Diane. Taking Up the Runes. New York: Red Wheel, 2005.

Paxon, Diane. Essential Asatru. New York: Kensington Publishing Co., 2006.

Peschel, Lisa. A Practical Guide to the Runes. St. Paul: Llewellyn Publishing, 1989.

Pennick, Nigel. The Pagan Book of Days. Rochester: Destiny Books, 1992.

Rael, Joseph. Being and Vibration. Tulsa: Council Oak Books, 1993.

Rose, H.J. Handbook of Greek Mythology. New York: Dutton and Co., 1959.

Rossman, Douglas "Dag". The Nine Worlds: A Dictonary of Norse Mythology. Bloomington: Scandisk, 2000.

Sams, Jamie and Carson, David. <u>Medicine Cards</u>. Santa Fe: Bear and Co, 1988.

Sams, Jamie. <u>Dancing the Dream</u>. New York: Harper, 1999.

Schlain, Leonard. <u>The Alphabet Versus the Goddess</u>. New York: Viking Press, 1998.

Scott, Michael. <u>Irish Folk and Fairy Tales Onmibus</u>. New York: Penguin, 1983.

Starhawk. <u>Spiral Dance</u>. New York: Harper Collins, 1979.

Stein, Diane. <u>The Kwan Yin Book of Changes</u>. St. Paul: Llewellyn, 1989.

Stein, Diane. <u>Essential Reiki.</u> Freedom, CA: The Crossing Press, 1995.

Stokker, Kathleen. <u>Remedies and Rituals: Folk Medicine in Norway and the New Land.</u> St. Paul: Minnesota Historical Society Press, 2007.

Stone, Merlin. <u>When God Was a Woman</u>. Orlando: Harcourt, Brace and Company. 1976.

Sturluson, Snorri. <u>The Prose Edda: Tales from Norse Mythology</u>. New York: Penguine Press, 2005.

Tacitus. <u>The Complete Works.</u> Translated by Church and Brodribb. New York: Random House, 1942.

Tauring, Kari C. <u>Little Rune Book</u>. Minneapolis: Homepress, 2003.

Tauring, Kari C. <u>Volva Stav Manual.</u> lulu.com, 2010

Thorsson, Edred. <u>Futhark: A Handbook of Rune Magic</u>. San Fransico: Weiser Books, 1983.

Trinkuunas, Jonas. Of Gods and Holidays: The Baltic Heritage. Lithuania, 1999.

Tzu, Lao. The Tao Te Ching. New York: Vintage Press, 1997.

Wodening, Eric. We Are Our Deeds: The Elder Heathenry it's Ethic and Thew. Watertown: THEOD, 1998.

Nelson Personal Study Text Bible. Revised Standard Version. Nashville: Thomas Nelson Bible Publishers, 1972.

Erdman's Family Encyclopedia of the Bible. Grand Rapids: Wm B. Erdman's Publishing Co., 1978

Web Resources (2016) Include:

www.germanicmythology.com (the most complete collection of Germanic/Nordic Mythology - writings and art - original language and side by side translations)

www.nordic-life.org (Yves Kodratoff)

www.sunnyway.com/runes/origins.html

www.phoenicia.org/alphabet.html

www.vikinganswerlady.com

members.tripod.com/IdunnasGrove

www.omniglot.com

www.thetroth.org

(Excellent sites by Maria Kvilhaug, Norway)

www.youtube.com/user/LadyoftheLabyrinth

www.freya.theladyofthelabyrinth.com/

(Excellent sites by Guðrún Kristín Magnúsdóttir, Iceland)

www.youtube.com/user/Goiagodi/videos

https://odsmal.org/

My research has led me through volumes of folk songs and stories that illuminate the beliefs and rituals of relationship with "the Nature" and all her beings. Special thanks to the musicians and scholars who continue to preserve this material, especially Agnes Buen Gårnas, Telemark, Norway and Mike and Else Sevig, Bloomington, Minnesota, US.

Milton Keynes UK
Ingram Content Group UK Ltd.
UKHW011307131223
434298UK00001B/408